Heart Reconciled

The Journey to a Whole & Integrated Heart

Heart Reconciled

The Journey to a Whole & Integrated Heart

Dr. Conrad A. Davies

Heart Reconciled:
The Journey to a Whole & Integrated Heart

Davies & Associates, LLC
info@daviesassociatesllc.com
Lexington, KY 40515

ISBN (Print): 979-8-9854921-2-5

Illustrator and Writing Consultant:
Chelsea Wisley, info@daviesassociatesllc.com

Front and Back Cover Design:
Jordan Turner, info@daviesassociatesllc.com

ACKNOWLEDGEMENTS

I acknowledge all those who spent many minutes or hours with me as I shared about the deep matters of my heart. Thank you for your grace in listening to and pondering my thoughts.

I want to thank my wife, **Kandace**, for listening to me most and for releasing me to write my books at just the right time. I love you, bless you, and honor you. You are the exact person the Lord knew I needed.

I acknowledge my kiddos, **CJ, Levi, and Sarah** for always cheering Daddy on in the work that I do. I trust I will continually be the best dad you guys have ever known. May the Lord use the best parts of me to show you how much He loves you. Everything good I have is from Him. I love you guys.

I honor you, **Chelsea Wisley,** for being willing to be my writing consultant and discern through my rawness. I have learned so much from you, and you have drawn out parts of me that only a skilled and gifted writing consultant could have done. I bless you in your gift to "speak Conrad" and help me speak more pastorally instead of academically. Thank you.

I acknowledge many of my **Brothers and Sisters** in the faith for being so dear to me during times when I needed to process things in my heart at deep levels. I honor the grace of God on your lives.

I bless you, my **Readers**. I hope will see and experience the power of how God changed me through this work. May the same be for you. In fact, may you have an even greater experience than I did.

I bless and honor the One and Only **King of Glory** who has entrusted me with this work. May He show us all our place in His Kingdom, and may He get the glory for His story. May this work lead us all to deeper levels of relationship with Him.

DEDICATION

This book is dedicated to all those whom the Lord has entrusted to us to help bring peace to their lives. May the peace of the Lord rest on you.

Friend, let's welcome God Almighty to make us into everything He intended for us to be.

Heart Reconciled

The Journey to a Whole & Integrated Heart

Dr. Conrad A. Davies

Table of Contents

FOREWORD

I knew about Dr. Conrad Davies long before I knew him. For years, I'd heard his name pop up in various circles, always in a positive light, typically in conjunction with either a teaching role or some type of work related to the word "reconciliation". Every time I heard about him, it stirred questions and curiosity within me. Who was this man who had so many connections with a myriad of individuals and organizations in my city? Why did so many people seem to be so deeply impacted by his words and his work? And what even was "reconciliation work" anyway?

I'll admit that when I finally met Conrad, I found myself struggling to categorize him. As a lifelong learner myself with a passion for understanding who people are and how they work, I had become accustomed over time to utilizing certain categorizations to help me really understand a person, to make sense of what made them tick, to predict how they might respond in a given situation. My system had served me well for a long time. But I realized fairly quickly that Conrad didn't fit in many, if any, of my trusty categorical boxes. Little did I know then that the journey of getting to know Conrad and his amazing family was about to disrupt so many of my long-held frameworks.

In the years I've known Conrad, I've had the privilege of learning from him in many capacities, both auditorily and experientially. In various seasons and settings, I've known him as teacher, prophetic voice, colleague, father figure, discipler, brother, and friend. In each role, I have seen him consistently embodying his God-given identity and encouraging others to do the same. He loves Jesus fiercely, he listens to the heart of his Father, and he humbly allows Holy Spirit to speak and work through him. He is a faithful son of the King, and he knows what it means to live loved and to allow that love to overflow.

You will see, hear, and feel that love, the Father's love, on the pages of this book. Friends, this book is special. I know no other like it. Much like its author, I can find no category for it. I am confident that it will be used by the Lord to teach you, challenge you, convict you, intrigue you, stir you, comfort you, invite you, fill you with hope, and draw out parts of yourself that you never knew existed. It has been prayed over. It has been wept over. It has been labored over. I've watched Conrad follow Holy Spirit's leading to dig deeper within himself, to share more vulnerably, to give of himself sacrificially in hopes that you, his Readers, will gain understanding of your own hearts and be spurred on to pursue Jesus more intimately.

Chances are, if you found yourself feeling drawn to this book, there is a hunger inside of you…a hunger to taste and see more of God, to experience His healing in your heart, to manifest true freedom in how you live. I know that same hunger. I remember over a year ago, when I first learned of the heart departments from Conrad and began to engage the Lord with questions about my own heart, I was blown away by the rapid transformation that began within me. The same concepts you will read about in this book launched me into a season of discovery, purification, growth, and above all, intimacy with Holy Spirit like never before. The journey has been one of tearing down old frameworks to make space for the new, embracing the unknown because I can trust that I am known by the trustworthy One who created and now reveals the depths of my own intricate, multifaceted, beautifully cherished heart. I can genuinely say that I am a changed person today because of the ways I've now learned to view and approach matters of the heart. By God's grace, you will too.

As a writing consultant for this book, I have gotten a closer look than most at everything that went into birthing this work. Tackling a topic as complex as the human heart is no small endeavor, and I can attest that it has also been costly. Saying yes to writing this book has required total submission to God's journey of refinement, and it is a journey that Conrad has not only obeyed the Lord in, but fully embraced. As you embark on your own journey, be assured that you have a humble yet confident and experienced guide in your author. Every single question Conrad invites you to ask the Lord has already been wrestled through in the quiet place between him and his Father. He is a gifted teacher, but also a willing student, submitting to the great Author of his own story, ever learning and posturing himself to receive more from God so he can give away more to others.

So, I invite you, Friends, to also take a posture of receiving from our brother. This gift he is giving you is about to turn your world upside down in the best way. It is indeed a gift, but it will require something of you. You may have to lay down preconceived notions, stretch your comfort levels past their breaking points, or even fully tear down lifelong frameworks, as I did. But what you will gain will far outweigh whatever God calls you to leave behind. Embrace the journey to understanding your heart, to discovering all that He put inside of you and its purposes for your life and His mission. I am certain you will be richly blessed as you do.

Chelsea Wisley
Writing Consultant

INTRODUCTION

Hello, Friend.

This book has the potential to transform your life.

I ask you to prayerfully consider my words, discerning with the Lord what you need and don't need right now. I ask that you listen for the Holy Spirit's insights, interpretations, teaching, and leadings. I encourage you to use this book as a helpful tool to see things more clearly, since your heart is the most important element of your life.

My comments may be considered new and unique to you, so I ask that you weigh them carefully before the Lord. My research seeks to utilize biblical themes to simplify the complexity of the human heart, enabling us to see God's beautiful purpose for our lives more clearly. I believe that there are clues, insights, plans, counsel, and purposes buried within our hearts, and we may not yet have the understanding, discernment, or knowledge to navigate the things that are so deep within.

Please join me on this journey to explore the inner workings of the heart, discover answers, and uncover some of the purposes of God for you. Many people are seeking their purpose, identity, and calling, and thankfully, God is faithful to communicate with us through clues within to help us. Thus, the goal of this work is to provide a framework for viewing the human heart and offer some exercises that can help us learn from God about the heart.

I hope you are ready for the adventure of a lifetime and are willing to engage in a process of change. This study has changed my perspective of how I view humanity, for I now understand God's ways more clearly. The journey of learning about the heart is like using a treasure map to find the hidden gems God has placed within you.

Are you willing to come on this journey with me? Let's explore the depths of what's inside of you and me, knowing that Holy Spirit will need to take us there. All He asks of us is for our willingness to gain understanding.

The Lord continually challenges me with the concepts you'll read about, and I trust that we will learn from them together. I don't claim to be an expert, yet I have asked the Lord to make me a man of understanding, as described in Proverbs 20:5, "The purpose in a man's heart is like deep water, but a man of understanding will draw it out."

Here is my prayer for us:

> *Lord, You are faithful to reveal and show us Your ways. May we not be overwhelmed by the depths of our hearts, but rest in Your peace, knowing that we can be people of understanding who can draw out the depths.*
>
> *Lord, may we have understanding.*
> *Lord, may we have wisdom and revelation to know what to do.*
> *Lord, may your grace empower us.*
> *Lord, open the eyes of our hearts and enlighten us.*
>
> *Holy Spirit, lead and guide us along the way. May Your peace that surpasses all understanding guard our hearts and minds in the knowledge of Jesus. Amen.*

I trust my prayers will stir you to want to go deeper with the Lord.

If you need any further help on the journey, please reach out.

Your Brother and Coach,

Dr. Conrad A. Davies
conrad@daviesassociatesllc.com

Davies & Associates, LLC
Training & Coaching
http://daviesassociatesllc.com

Be Reconciled Lexington, Inc.
501(c)(3) Nonprofit Organization
http://bereconciledlexington.org

Chapter One

HOLY SPIRIT AND LISTENING PRAYER

God graciously made some decisions for our benefit.

God revealed His grace to us by deciding to fix the core problems of humanity. He decided to give humans a choice to love Him or not, rather than making us as puppets with Him "controlling our strings." He decided to create a legal system that provided a means to identify sin, give us access back to Him when we are separated, and relieve our guilt and shame. He decided to provide an ultimate sacrifice of Himself through Jesus Christ to take the punishment we should have received. He decided, for those who receive and accept Jesus, to give us His Holy Spirit to live inside of us.

His works and His ways are so gracious.

When I was 18 years old, I was told about how gracious God was to humanity and how I have access to Him because of what He did for us. I believed that message during my second semester of college. I remember so clearly the beauty of Holy Spirit[1] resting upon me, and I wept like a little child for about 20 minutes. It was a glorious night.

I need to take a moment to share my lens of who Holy Spirit is before discussing matters about the heart. Too often teachings on Holy Spirit are distant and impersonal, full of abstract and religious "Christianese" language that minimizes His character. I want to open up a perspective of how near, close, personal, gentle, and powerful Holy Spirit is in our lives, if we will let Him have His way with us.

I grew up in a denomination that did not talk about Holy Spirit as a personal close companion whom I could learn from, walk with, receive power from, or engage. It seemed like Holy Spirit was a cognitively acknowledged part of the Trinity of God, but was not personally connected to me. The focus was Jesus and His work on the cross. The

[1] I regularly use "Holy Spirit" instead of "the Holy Spirit" because it is my way of referencing Him personally instead of as an impersonal entity. There is nothing wrong with using "the" before Holy Spirit, yet it can connote an impersonal connection. As a result, I am intentional to remove "the" because I want to express how separate He is from every other spirit. He is Holy and set apart.

focus was also God as Creator and as the One who determined everything, yet there was very little discussion about or engagement with Holy Spirit, the One who dwells within the believer. The denomination had quite a works-based orientation and the focus was on good, benevolent human effort to satisfy God's expectations for humanity. I don't agree with that position now; however, that was my context.

After I gave my life to Jesus (a story which I'll later share in full), I learned and discovered that Holy Spirit is so close and personal. I experienced firsthand what Jesus meant when He promised to send us the gift of Holy Spirit. Holy Spirit is so tender, sensitive, powerful, near, comforting, helpful, insightful, and the best researcher on the planet. He knows exactly how to convict at the right moment, and He is serious about His role in the life of the believer. He wants to help, aid, comfort, and counsel you and me in our life journey. For this reason, much of my commentary in the next few paragraphs will be discoveries I have had through my own personal experiences with Holy Spirit as well as from the Scriptures. I admit that my perspective is my own human viewpoint, and so I ask you to take what I say and go before the Lord in your own way to evaluate what I share with you. I trust as you and I go before the Lord together, we will both learn from Holy Spirit and get the best about our lives revealed to us.

HOLY SPIRIT AND THE HEART

You are about to read a book about the matters within your heart. One perspective from Scripture is that the heart is:

> "...deceitful above all things, and desperately sick; who can understand it? I the Lord search the heart and test the mind, to give every man according to his ways, according to the fruit of his deeds..." (Jeremiah 17:9-10).

If Jeremiah emphasizes that the human heart is diseased, God has to do a work to change it, heal it, and transform it. In other words, we need a heart transplant so that we can have a viable, healthy, functional heart in order to move forward in life. The good news is that God provided an available heart for any person who wants it if they believe in Jesus' work on the cross. At the point of their belief, the transplant is immediate, and they can begin to live a new life in Christ. Any and all broken hearts can be transplanted with a new, God-healed heart.

As I stated in my story above, on the night I wept for about 20 minutes after saying "yes" to Jesus, I recognized that my life was changed. *I received my heart transplant.* I knew something felt different in me and that I was able to move forward in my life even after the pains, hurts, disappointments, frustrations, and confusions I had encountered thus far. I knew that I could regularly walk with God and come close to Him. It was intuitive and natural, yet I needed some teaching on how to fully live my new life because in the days to follow, something strange started happening in me.

I quickly learned that just like a medical heart transplant patient, I also needed to build new daily habits to sustain this new life. When an individual receives a physiological heart transplant patient, they have to take an immunosuppressant medication every day for the rest of their life because the body does not like the new foreign heart. Their immune system views the new heart as a threat. If they miss even one day of medication, the body will reject the transplanted heart. Similarly, my sinful nature fought against this new spiritual heart that I received from the Lord. My daily medication had to be prayer and the Word of God in reading the scriptures. I had to change my lifestyle habits, for I was in a daily battle for my new spiritual life. It was a life and death journey then, and it still continues to be. The Apostle Paul's words to the Galatians are a regular reminder:

> "So I say, walk by the Spirit, and you will not gratify the desires of the flesh. For the flesh desires what is contrary to the Spirit, and the Spirit what is contrary to the flesh. They are in conflict with each other, so that you are not to do whatever you want" (Galatians 5:16-17, NIV).

I did not understand walking by the Spirit at first, but over the years, especially after I unpacked the revelation of medical heart transplant patients, I realized that walking with Holy Spirit is a game changer. Holy Spirit leaves me extremely vulnerable, but He comforts me. Holy Spirit regulates my life, especially when I feel out of sorts. Holy Spirit will intervene and intercede on my behalf, particularly when I am weak. Holy Spirit will lead, guide, and grant me wisdom, especially when I don't know what to do or where to go. He becomes the protector of my life, and I continually learn to become increasingly dependent on Him.

Holy Spirit knows the most tender parts of my heart and will reveal what is happening within, even when it's deeper and more mysterious than my own understanding of my internal state. Holy Spirit will take me to dimensions of change at levels that only He can, and I have to trust what He is doing inside of me when it does not make sense.

Friend, I share all of this because what you are about to learn about the inner workings of your heart will bring you to deeper levels of intimacy with Holy Spirit. You will begin to see the beauty of who you are. The majority of our discussions will make the most sense in partnership with Holy Spirit. The Bible says that Holy Spirit "searches everything, even the depths of God."[2] If Holy Spirit has that capacity to search the depths of God, how much more does He have the capacity to know you and me? Our gracious God has given us the most precious gift of Holy Spirit through Jesus' work on the cross. We need Holy Spirit.

The more I speak about Holy Spirit, the more I want to emphasize that He is the part of God who dwells in the believer as a deposit guaranteeing our inheritance to come.[3] I engage Holy Spirit in a variety of ways, such as scripture reading, fellowship with other Christians filled with God's Spirit, and various kinds of prayers, especially listening prayer. I want to take a moment and introduce you to how engage Him through regular listening prayer.

LISTENING PRAYER

I regularly hear and discern God's voice through a method of "listening prayer." Whether I want to hear His heart about a matter, or I need His perspective or answers about a situation, or I am in prayer about someone else, my go-to is listening prayer. While Scripture establishes how I learn about God's nature and character, I need more on how to act, process, or respond to particular things happening in my life. In other words, I believe Scripture shows us sufficient themes and patterns of how God engages humanity, however, we need help from Holy Spirit on how to practically and properly apply biblical principles to our current lives. For me, I have learned to spend most of my quiet time with the Lord, reading, pondering, and asking Him all sorts of questions. I'd rather listen to Him than always pray about what I think I know. I want to live by what Moses and Jesus said about God, "...man does not live by bread alone, but by every word that comes from the mouth of the Lord."[4]

---

[2] 1 Corinthians 2:10, "...these things God has revealed to us through the Spirit. For the Spirit searches everything, even the depths of God."

[3] Ephesians 1:13-14

[4] Deuteronomy 8:3 and Matthew 4:4

My desire is to listen to God's Word and allow it to be a continual meditation and focus of my life.

I want to live life according to King David's amazing revelation in Psalm 139 on how much there is to learn from God. David reveals that there is a book written about us. He also reveals that God's thoughts are more than the grains of sand of the sea. That's a lot of thoughts. David also sees God's thoughts as precious. Here is David's prayer in Psalm 139:15-18 (NIV):

> My frame was not hidden from you when I was made in the secret place, when I was woven together in the depths of the earth. Your eyes saw my unformed body; all the days ordained for me were written in your book before one of them came to be. How precious to me are your thoughts, God! How vast is the sum of them! Were I to count them, they would outnumber the grains of sand when I awake, I am still with you.

In my world, I've learned to value God's thoughts as more precious than my thoughts. I recognize that the foundation of my life was not originally built on God's perspective, but on cultural traditions and patterns that did not honor the Lord. Some of my default patterns clash with God and seem right in my eyes but have truly led me to destruction.[5] I think poorly sometimes. Therefore, it is more worth my time to focus and seek after God's thoughts than to get caught up in my own. He is the author of my life. He knows my story and my journey. He knows the beauty of revelation and knows the power of living by His words from His mouth.

In light of these truths, our journey of learning about what's happening inside of us will incorporate spending important time with God in relationship. I suggest a journaling method to record yours and His thoughts. I will provide listening prayer prompts for your journaling so that you can hear from God and process what is being revealed. As 1 Corinthians 2:10 tells us, the Holy Spirit "searches out the deep things of God." When we come to Him with our questions, we can be assured that He will also search out our hearts and will bring revelation regarding what we need to know.

There will be some regular consistent questions that will lead much of our listening prayer prompts in each section. While some other questions may be more general or specific, and some will ask you to go

---

[5] Proverbs 14:12

deeper, ask about what to do or ask the Lord to show you your role in the situation. Here are some examples, listed next to their question type:

General: Lord, what do You want to say to me?
Specific: Lord, what do You want to say to me about my XYZ situation?
Supplemental: Lord, what else do I need to know?
Action: Lord, how do I partner with You?
Framework: Lord, what is my role in this situation?

When we practice listening prayer in this book, please consider a few things:

1. You are speaking to **the King** of the Universe who created all things of Himself, for Himself, and by Himself. He is the Lord, the Boss, and the Head of all life. You and I have been granted the grace to know Him through the work of Jesus on the cross. We have been given the privilege to know Him. He deserves the utmost respect, especially when He's speaking.

2. **He is a Father** who wants to help you and identify you. He has good intentions and knows you better than any other person in the universe.

3. **Your posture is that of a scribe.** A scribe is a writer and record-keeper. One role of a scribe is to record the thoughts of a king. I recommend that you take God's words seriously, embrace each word as precious, and make His words worthy of your attention.

4. **God wants** to communicate[6] with you. You might get visions, images, simple words, phrases, whole paragraphs or pages of information, or other senses/feelings. God will communicate in a way specific to you to best pass along meaning and insight to you.

5. When you finish your journaling, take whatever you wrote down and **evaluate it**. Before you act on anything you hear, compare it to the nature and character of God in the Bible. **Process and pray** through your writings regularly with your Bible-believing Christian community.

---

[6] I use the word "communicate" throughout the book because God does not only just "speak" to us, but He has many forms of communication to help us understand His heart and to move us along in our lives.

Through this listening prayer method, you are welcoming God to communicate to you about His perspective of your life. It also allows for two-way communication, rather than you simply talking to or at Him through prayer and then assuming you know what God is saying to you. This exercise tends to help individuals receive clarity in their relationship with Him and others. One of the most important parts of the listening prayer process is that you have something to work with that can be discerned through Scripture, shared with your Christian community, and processed over time without forgetting it. With time and discipline, you will find yourself testing, approving, and discerning what God is communicating to your heart.[7] This method is a beautiful practice for hearing the Lord's heart and learning from Him.

As we start our journey, let me pray:

> *King Jesus, You are the author of our lives, and You know us better than anyone else. I thank You for the grace You give to us to hear and know the heart of God. Thank You for giving us access to Holy Spirit.*
>
> *Holy Spirit, I ask for Your wisdom and revelation to rest upon us. I ask for You to lead us as children. I ask You for Your counsel and might. I ask that You would increase our knowledge of who God is and increase the fear of the Lord within us. Teach us all the things we need to know.*
>
> *Father God, thank You that our story was written in Your book before any of the words came to be. Will you reveal Your will for our lives? Will You show us Your intentions? Will You speak to us and show us who we are? You are so gracious, merciful, and faithful.*
>
> *I bless our journey, and I thank You for the revelation of Your purposes that You buried deep in our hearts. I ask these things, in Jesus' name.*

[7] Romans 12:1-2

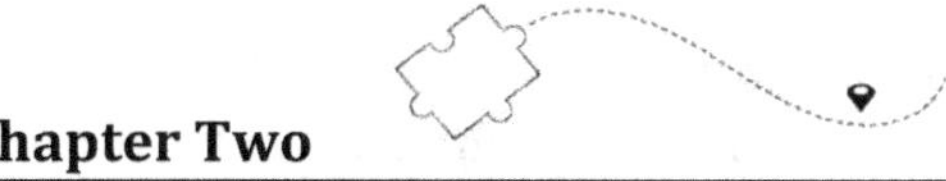

Chapter Two

"YOU SOUND LIKE A 15-YEAR-OLD BOY"

In my Christian walk, there were quiet moments without much conflict, as if life were flowing smoothly. I perceived that my wife and I were on a trajectory of living the good, normal American Christian lifestyle: going to church regularly, praying, and reading our Bibles. Yet, in one particular season of my marriage, when I thought I was okay, Holy Spirit interrupted my world to take me deeper in relationship with Him.

To get some assistance with some marital conflict, my wife and I invited a couple who served as our parenting and marriage mentors to come help us process. They discussed the matter with us, outlined some suggestions, and asked more questions. But then the tone of the conversation unexpectedly changed. As we continued the conversation, the mentor wife interjected at a particular moment, and in response to some of my comments, she exclaimed, "Conrad, you sound like a 15-year-old boy!"

I paused for a moment, internally wrestling with a potential offense. "What?! You calling me a 15-year-old boy?! I am a grown man, married with children."

She continued and explained how my response to the conflict sounded like I was addressing the situation as if I were still an egotistical, self-centered, 15-year-old boy, trying to blame shift the circumstance and to not take responsibility. I don't remember many of the details of the marital conflict, but I most remember the connection with the mentor wife because it had such an emotional impact on me. It was as if my mother were rebuking me but, strangely, **loving me**.

In that moment, I struggled with some deep emotional triggers.

She was challenging my paradigm, for I was in my late thirties and felt I had made much progress in my emotional and spiritual development. My ego was being confronted, and I began internally justifying myself by perceived "good deeds":

I'm mature because I've led Bible studies.
I have discipleship relationships, and I know the Lord intimately.

I have quiet times.
I read my Bible.
I have daily disciplines, and I go to church regularly.
I counsel people and help them in their Christian life.

How could she connect me to an immature 15-year-old boy?

What a blow to my ego!

What a blow to some of the deep things in my heart that I thought I had worked out!

What a blow to my perception of God's transforming power already at work in me!

How could she?!

I grew up in a world that had its fair share of emotional trauma, and I did not know that the residual of those experiences was bleeding into my marriage. I knew that I had grown from much of my past trauma, and I **thought** I was healed from most of these emotional wounds. I knew that I was God's son and that He was pleased with me, yet these comments from my mentor deeply disturbed me, ultimately starting me on a journey with that Lord that would eventually change my life. I just never expected that simple comments of comparison to a 15-year-old boy navigating marital conflict would bring such conviction and challenge to my heart.

Holy Spirit was communicating to me; He was grabbing my attention. Yet, I had a physical posture of disdain and frustration before our mentors, though I continued to listen as respectfully as I could manage.

A few moments later, while I was still processing the offense, the hurt, and the disrespect, our mentors went on to relate to my feelings with their personal stories of overcoming their own emotional immaturity at various moments in their lives. Their stories and humility brought me back to focus on their words, and they began to stabilize the emotional and intellectual parts of my heart. The wife gently encouraged me, saying, "Conrad, since you have such a well-developed intellect, you will be able to 'grow up' your emotions rather quickly."

Her words of encouragement disarmed the loads of tension I was experiencing. I acknowledge that my initial processing led me to feel helpless and hopeless, which triggered my frustration and pride walls to come up because I did not know what to do. Consider…our respected mentors with 40+ years of marriage experience were speaking about my immaturity in this marital conflict. Their words carried weight. Thankfully, they didn't just leave me with a rebuke, but they loved me by giving me some direction.

As I continued to process my initial offenses, I recognized that no one had ever taught me how to deal with the emotional part of my heart. I did not realize that *my intellect* could help 'grow up' my emotions. Though I initially felt helpless, I was suddenly feeling empowered and known because she had related to me and acknowledged my "well-developed intellect". Little did I know that this new concept of my intellect helping to grow up my emotions would become a theme in my life that would continue from that moment on.

How comforted I felt that a gracious God would overlook the evil in my heart when I didn't know the depth of what was happening! Pride had blinded me to think that because I was performing all the right Christian duties and knew I was growing in the Lord, I couldn't possibly be compared to a 15-year-old boy. This conversation helped me realize how deceitful, complex, deep, and interconnected the components of the heart can be. God had searched, judged, and revealed my heart. He looked beyond my offenses and began the release of new revelation that set me on a new trajectory of my life.

With comfort, encouragement, and a new found passion, I thought to myself, *"I can do this. I can grow up this 15-year-old boy."*

As the conversation ended, I appreciated and thanked them for their relatability, affirmations, love, and wisdom. I was reminded of and humbled by the scripture in Hebrews 12:7-8:

> "It is for discipline that you have to endure. God is treating you as sons. For what son is there whom his father does not discipline? If you are left without discipline, in which all have participated, then you are illegitimate children and not sons."

I thanked God that He would use them to show that I was not an illegitimate child of God but one whom God continuously wants to discipline and transform to look more like Him.

This conversation was the beginning of the revelation of this book. My hope in sharing my process of understanding my heart is to spark a desire in you to begin your own journey.

Friends, remember, the human heart is deep, deceitful, and complex, and we don't know it as well as we think we do. But with Holy Spirit's revelation and help, we can come to know so much more than we could ever uncover on our own. Let's explore the heart together.

CHAPTER TWO LISTENING PRAYER QUESTIONS

I encourage you to review the Holy Spirit and Listening Prayer chapter for reminders about how to conduct listening prayer, and then ask the Lord these questions:

1) Lord, what do You want to say to me regarding this chapter?

2) Lord, what is one thing You want to change in my heart?

3) Lord, what area of scripture do You want to bring to my heart to meditate on?

4) Lord, is there anything else You want to share with me?

Chapter Three

"YOU WON'T LET ME COMFORT YOU"

I need to share another story.

Years after the meeting with our mentors, my wife and I were in a church meeting one afternoon, and the pastor decided invite us to spend some quiet time in order to hear what the Lord wanted to say to us. This exercise was a normal activity during our weekly meetings.

Here is an excerpt from my listening prayer[8] journal entry that day during the meeting:

Lord, what do You want to say?

His response:

> **You won't let me comfort you. I want to comfort you.**
>
> **(Pause)**
>
> **I know it's hard and I know the struggle.**
>
> **Let the secret place be your favorite place.**
>
> **I am the comforter. I am the storyteller. I am the redeemer and lover of your soul. I am the provider and deliverer. I sustain you and keep you. I love you and hold you. I am the way maker.**
>
> **I want the best for you...**

The Lord interrupted my world with strong statements for the sake of change. He was moving me along in the journey of my heart, drawing out things that I would have never considered.

---

[8] This reference to listening prayer is the same method described in the Holy Spirit and Listening Prayer section of the first chapter. As a reminder, Christians often pray at God in a one-directional way rather than have a multi-directional prayer conversation with God. This method of listening prayer is a tool to slow down, listen, and evaluate what the Lord may be saying to us.

Of what I sensed from His heart, the first two sentences He said rattled me. I felt the depth of love and compassion in His tone in "You won't let me comfort you. I want to comfort you," yet I found my heart quickly retorting, "But, I *know* You as Comforter." I was somewhat confused as I pondered my first impression of this entry.

Though I did not write it in my journal, I sensed a gentle but firm response that would further unravel my life. Though not audible, my own spirit heard Holy Spirit clearly say:

I did not say that, Son...You won't *let* me comfort you.

What do you mean by "let", Lord?

In simple terms, the Lord was communicating to my heart that even though I cognitively knew Him as Comforter,[9] I did not let Him comfort me. I wrestled with the Lord's words for a few weeks.

Lord, why would You say that I won't let You comfort me?

Lord, I know your heart to comfort and I know You as Comforter. What am I missing?

What are You trying to communicate to me?

Through my weeks of wrestling, I recognized that the Lord was getting my attention, showing me that I had not allowed Him to enter those deeper places of my heart. The quest was now continuing in ways that were unexpected, uncomfortable, gut-wrenching, and somewhat confusing.

I recognized that my cognition, my perspective, and my prideful conclusions I lived in were being dismantled. From first being challenged to grow up this internal 15-year-old boy to now this, God was engaging me at a level that I did not have a grid for processing. My King, my Lord, my Lover, and my Savior was loving me well by revealing the deep things of my heart that only understanding could draw out. Remember, Proverbs 20:5 says:

---

[9] This is based on the Gospel of John 14:26, "But the Comforter, which is the Holy Ghost, whom the Father will send in my name, he shall teach you all things, and bring all things to your remembrance, whatsoever I have said unto you (KJV)."

> "The purpose in a man's heart is like deep water, but a man of understanding will draw it out."

I wanted to become a man of understanding, and these conversational moments with the Lord stirred a quest to learn of what He was communicating and doing in my heart. In my pursuit, I studied the Hebrew words for heart: lev and levav. I traced and categorized how these words were used throughout the Old Testament. I did the same with the Greek word for heart, kardia, examining its use throughout the New Testament. I made charts of how the words were used in their respective contexts. My research journey sparked a season of growth for me as I sought the Lord fervently.

I prayed.
I asked questions.
I processed my thoughts with my brothers and sisters.
I studied.
I recorded my thoughts.
I humbled myself before the Lord.

I even went so far as studying the heart as the physical organ, such as the nature of the scientific discovery of heart transplants. Those discoveries gave me metaphorical implications of why God needed to give us new hearts.[10]

I discovered that the heart is deceitful, deep, complex, and regularly needs to be examined.

I discovered that the heart is like soil and needs to be tended and nourished.

I discovered that the heart is like a "Central Headquarters" of a massive business organization, and it has unique departments that are intended to work interdependently with one another.

I couldn't get enough of what I was learning. The more I learned, the more I wanted to know.

---

[10] Ezekiel 11:19-20: "And I will give them one heart, and a new spirit I will put within them. I will remove the heart of stone from their flesh and give them a heart of flesh, that they may walk in my statutes and keep my rules and obey them. And they shall be my people, and I will be their God."

As my understanding increased, my hunger grew with it. It consumes me to this day.

My hope is that the fruit of my story in this book can transform your perspective and the way you live, if you continue on the journey with me. There are purposes of your life that are too deep for you, and only intimacy with Holy Spirit and the understanding He gives can reveal it.

CHAPTER THREE LISTENING PRAYER QUESTIONS

1) Lord, what are You saying to me related to this chapter?

2) Lord, what is happening in my heart?

3) Lord, do I allow You to comfort me?

4) Lord, where are those places in my heart where I cognitively know You, yet You want more?

5) Lord, what else do You want to say to me?

Chapter Four

MY CONVICTIONS AND DISCOVERIES

The Bible shows us the nature and the character of God.

Throughout story after story, God interacts with humans by showing His faithfulness, His loving-kindness, and His tenderness to who we are. God also demonstrates that He is holy and just; He is the authority over all authorities on the planet. God has a range in His characteristics. As I mentioned previously, one characteristic of God that has stood out in this season of my life is that **God is a Comforter**.

As I unpacked some of my childhood trauma, I recognized that deposits were made in my heart that were not good for me. As a naive and vulnerable child, I had a number of poor foundations laid in my life, resulting in my younger self looking for comfort in all the wrong places. I attempted to navigate life with false comforts, insecurities, and lies. A look into my family history gives context to understand how and why these struggles came to be.

NOT COVERED AND NOT TRAINED

In the early 1970's, my immigrant parents came to the United States with a dream in mind to make life better for themselves. This new country offered promises educationally, financially, and opportunistically that were not accessible to them in their home country. Thus, in their early twenties, my parents left their home with one-way tickets to come to the United States. Their vision was strong, yet the hurts, pains, and brokenness in their own hearts were unhealed.

They came as potential heroes in their families by getting away, but they did not realize that they were about to expose themselves to isolation from community, intense fears, more rejection, and prideful attempts to keep their dignity. On their quest, they started in Kentucky, moved to the east coast, came to Southern Illinois, and returned back to Kentucky. They were driven. After about 15 total years of an educational journey, they completed a combined total of seven university degrees, and they both finally started working substantively.

During those years, they birthed and raised three children, of which I am the middle child.

My parents' journey included a great deal of delayed gratification, poverty, and broken hopes and dreams. Looking back now, I can see much of their internal struggle that was unclear to me at that time: unhealthy interactions, untended areas of their hearts, and an increase of what I call "pride masks" to cover the shame that ruled them. Consequently, everything became a fight. They fought for dignity. They fought each other. They fought other people. They fought for us kids. They fought for their sanity. They fought for their dreams.

They were so focused on their dreams and passions that no one would have known the depth of what was happening in their hearts. I don't think they knew the depth of what was happening in their hearts. It was as if they were on autopilot and just living life based on what they were told would bring success. They were striving to make their journey work according to what the "promise" was supposed to be. Yet, as Solomon says in Proverbs 20:5, "The purposes of the heart are like deep waters..." As I've prayed and sought to discern why my parents lived the way they did, I've concluded that perhaps my parents were floating on the surface of what was in their hearts, which is what fueled their agendas. I don't believe they understood the depth of what was inside of their hearts.

Despite their intense passion to move to the United States in search of a better life, these two immigrants **did not have any idea how to deal with their deep internal heart challenges**. How, then, were they to guide and train their children in how to deal with their own hearts?

In my adult years, the above question gave me compassion for my parents. We simply can't give what we don't have.

As you might imagine, my dad focused us on education and sports, which became "pride masks" to cover deep-seated shame. My experience with my academic pursuits and my sports training couldn't really train certain parts of my heart. I learned how to cover the less developed parts of my heart with intellect, false humility, false comforters, and the quest for the American dream. I numbed any feelings that were uncomfortable. I craved addictive behaviors that made me feel better. I longed for a hopeful future of great successes, while living in great shame. In all of this, I was unaware of the depth of what was happening inside of me.

Fortunately, I have always loved to learn, which gave promise and willingness to experience different journeys of discovery and change, yet

I did not have tools to work on my heart. Many places of my heart were underdeveloped. I was simply not placed in environments or given frameworks that taught me how to live life fully with a whole heart.

I would like to clarify that the above statements about my parents are not meant to place blame on them, but rather are intended to simply reveal a missing aspect of my life. As a parent myself, my parents' story challenges me to deal with my internal heart issues even more because my children need me to give them something I now actually possess: **a lifestyle of letting the Lord continually help me tend to the garden of my heart and comfort me during the challenges of life**.

NAIVE AND VULNERABLE

When I went off to college, I attended the same school as my parents and older sibling had, not realizing that the Lord was going to use my school experiences to change my life. One experience included playing in a fairly intense Division One college soccer program that challenged much of my emotional stability; I had a load of difficult moments as a college athlete. Another experience included the demands of a chemistry degree program supported by a national chemical society that gave me a four-year scholarship. One other experience included being humbled from the boasting of what I thought my life was supposed to be: working as a food chemist of some prominent national company. In my ignorance, I was living life with various 'pride masks,' or as I sometimes call them, 'pride makeup,' and I was hiding behind my achievements. I did not realize the Lord was about to use these experiences to realign my life and lead me to his purposes.

I, therefore, used my platforms as 'pride makeup' to cover my shame, fear, blemishes, insecurities, inadequacies, and vulnerabilities. I embraced being a Division One athlete by training myself to be one of the strongest and most fit players on the team. I boasted and told everyone about my chemistry major, math minor, and future plans to work in the chemistry field. I even boasted about not having to pay for school because of the academic, soccer, and chemistry scholarships I earned. My goal was to recreate myself at the university by escaping my hometown experiences and family issues. I was able to start fresh with new experiences and new relationships with people who did not know me. Getting away from home and gaining success elsewhere was an opportunity to make myself look like what I imagined for myself, especially since no one knew my real story.

Then, in came Holy Spirit, interrupting my prideful, image-driven life, and He began drawing me to Jesus.

During my second semester at the university as I was in one of my calculus courses, I noticed this girl in class who grabbed my attention. I learned of her name and began a relationship with her. She was a believer in Jesus and invited me to come with her to participate in a new Bible study on campus. I went, not really for my own spiritual growth, but because I liked the girl.

Something started happening inside of my heart each time I heard the preached Word at the study, and I kept feeling convicted that I was not living up to my best. I began to realize that I needed to change; yet, I did not know how. One day, as I was wrestling with guilt from sin I had just committed, I heard a Christian song from a popular artist. The song spoke about the comfort of God in the face of our past mistakes. Recognizing that I was out of my depths, I asked my friend to call our Bible study leader because I needed help. He answered rather quickly and told me to come to his room to chat.

I didn't realize that my life was about to change. The Comforter who had been pursuing me all my life was about to give me a warm embrace.

In my naivety and vulnerability, I didn't know how much makeup I was wearing to cover my inadequacies and shame. All I knew was that I was an eager 18-year-old kid wanting to do something great in life.

I did not realize how much hurt, pain, brokenness, wounds, and scars were causing turmoil within my heart.

I did not realize how much I was truly crying out for comfort from the fear, rejection, and shame.

I did not realize that I needed Jesus to be my Savior.

I was now about to encounter the living God through a gospel presentation, and I had no idea the depth of the love God had for me.

I went to the Bible study leader's room on that brisk cold night in February 1999, and I checked in at the front desk of the residence hall for him to come down and get me. He welcomed me up to his room, and after some brief small talk, he proceeded to ask me what was going on. I shared with him what had happened that night, and he began to share with me the good news that God had a plan to fix humanity's brokenness through the life of Jesus. The leader used a small, printed booklet with diagrams to show me about my separation from God and how Jesus was the bridge to get reconnected back to God.

My heart was now stirred, for I knew I needed my brokenness fixed.

At the end of the booklet, there was a prayer of salvation that I could pray if I wanted God's answer. My Bible study leader invited me to pray that prayer, if I was ready. I did not know at the time that that scripted prayer was about to open my heart to a world with Jesus I could have never imagined. I began to slowly read the prayer. I only made it through the first few words and began to weep:

"Lord Jesus, thank You for dying for me..."

I wept for the next 20 minutes because God's love overwhelmed me. I finally let Him come in and take residence in my life. It unlocked the floodgates of many emotions. His love began casting out the fear in my heart. His love began cleansing and removing the "pride-makeup." His love replaced a stony heart and gave me a heart responsive to Him. I found myself so vulnerable and more eager to offer my life to Him to use me for His purposes, even though I did not know what would happen next.

That day, **the Lord replaced my heart and gave me a new one that wanted to love Him, serve Him, and make Him known to others**.

That day simply started the journey of learning how to trust Him.

FALSE COMFORTERS WHO BEFRIENDED ME

After that day, I had no idea what I had signed up for.

I didn't know that the war had just begun...

The war to offer my body as a living sacrifice to God.
The war to fight against the natural bent of my sinful nature.
The war to fight the good fight of faith.
The war to allow Him to purify my heart so that I can see and experience God.
The war to keep persevering when my faith was being tested.

The war began because all of the false comforting spirits who were familiar, seemingly innocent and friendly, were now being fired as the managers in my heart. I did not know or understand that I had welcomed these other spirits into my life. Now that I had let Holy Spirit come in, these other spirits were being challenged to leave. These false comforters were, in reality, evil spirits who feasted on the darkness in which I was living. They came alongside me to give me counterfeit ways to comfort myself and not allow God and others to comfort me in healthy ways. Holy Spirit wanted to be my chief Comforter, for I didn't know that God was jealous[11] for a relationship with me. I did not realize the internal war that began as a result of my decision to welcome in Holy Spirit as the new manager of my heart.

There were three particular spirits serving as the primary managers of different parts of my heart: spirits of pride, fear, and rejection. Pride provided false comfort by deceiving me into believing that if I just hid my real problems and attempted to control different areas of my life, then I would be okay. Spirits associated with fear deceived me by convincing me that I could fight for my belief systems, run from my problems, freeze in the midst of challenges, or people please in order to avoid someone becoming mad at me. Spirits connected to fear regularly reinforced my shame and insecurities. Rejection, and the spirits connected to it, communicated that I needed to find those people and places that appeared to accept me. Anyone who showed me attention, seemingly valued me, or affirmed my insecurities continued to nurse my wounds from rejection. Throughout most of my life, I had experienced foolishness, worthless things, or deceitful environments that fueled fear, pride, or rejection and allowed them to operate.

I felt I needed acceptance at any cost.

I experienced so many false comforters who communicated things to my heart to lie to me and identify me falsely. I did not know, nor did I understand how to know, about these sophisticated things. Out of that lack of knowledge, so many questions arose in my heart:

Who teaches us about our hearts and the different needs of the heart?

[11] The concept of jealousy connotes that God wants exclusivity in relationship with Him. He does not welcome mixture, inclusivity, or spiritual polygamy in our relationship. Some scriptural examples are Exodus 20:5; Exodus 34:14; Deut. 4:24; Deut. 5:9; and Deut. 6:15.

Where are the parents, teachers, and friends who will protectively intervene when they see us going down a poor direction?

Where are the people who have been comforted by the Lord and have the capacity to help others receive comfort?[12]

Consequently, the lies and stories told to me by these false comforters kept me anxious, bound, hiding, shameful, boastful, and afraid to be who I was really meant to be. I didn't know my true identity. My only long-term teacher up to this point had been my own experience, and it had not sufficiently prepared me for what I needed in order to become whole. I knew that my heart had broken pieces and needed healing. Since I was new in my relationship with the Lord, I had to learn over many years that He was the One with all of the answers. There were not people of understanding around me to help me. I needed connections made in ways to help me purify my heart so that I could see and experience God.

My desire for you, Friend, **is to help you go on a journey of purifying your heart by firing the long-held, spiritual managers and false comforters of your own heart**.

I want you to experience God in a way that fundamentally changes you.

As Matthew 5:8 says, "Blessed are the pure in heart, for they shall see God."

CHAPTER FOUR LISTENING PRAYER QUESTIONS

1) Lord, what is my story with You?

2) Lord, what do You want me to know about my story with You?

3) Lord, what spiritual managers or false comforters are in my heart?

4) Lord, how do You want to purify my heart? Will You give me Your wisdom and reveal to me what I need to know?

---

[12] 2 Corinthians 1:3-7

Chapter Five

CULTURAL PERSPECTIVES OF THE HEART

The goal of this section is to outline a dictionary perspective based on three cultural lenses for defining the heart, knowing that we need a foundation laid for the rest of the book. Each culture identified in this section would have a number of similarities and differences in the denotation of the word "heart," because sociocultural connotations influence perceptions. My desire is to expand our perspectives beyond the modern English definitions that are influenced by cultural philosophies that could alter perceptions. If there are any changes in the morality of a culture, there will be influences that can affect the interpretation and understanding of certain words or concepts. Consider how Noah Webster, an early lexiconist of the English language, would have viewed words during a time when the Bible informed and influenced much of American culture. Webster decided to incorporate biblical scriptures in his definitions. Similarly, the ancient Greeks and the Hebrews would have had different perspectives of the heart because of their cultural lenses. Let's dive in and work through these different perspectives together.

The heart is complex, and generations of cultures have attempted to bring clarity and definition to this thing we call "the heart." In this section, I want to briefly outline three cultural perspectives of the heart.

I won't bring emphasis to the definitions of the heart as an organ (as in, "the heart is a muscular organ that pumps blood"), or the definitions of the heart as the middle of something (for example, "the heart of the sea"). I instead want to emphasize the heart in the context of human lifestyle choices and how the heart is like a central headquarters of the human experience.

Let's begin with English-speaking cultures with influences of Western civilization.

ENGLISH DEFINITIONS OF THE HEART

If you were to do a Google search using artificial intelligence (AI) on "the heart," you are most likely going to receive a scientific definition of the biological functions of the heart. You'll learn about blood flow, oxygenation, chambers of the heart, and other aspects of its anatomical functions. You might have to dig a bit deeper to find some of the cultural perspectives of how the heart applies to life beyond our anatomy.

If you use a modern English dictionary,[13] you may find a number of definitions focused on only the emotional and feelings aspects of the heart, or the more abstract concepts like the drawing of a picture of a heart. The definition of heart, from an English perspective, does not give the best holistic picture of what is really inside of the human heart. Its non-robust explanation welcomes our culture to compartmentalize things away from the heart like our will, our thinking, our conscience, and our desires, all of which are included within the heart by more ancient cultures.

However, if we examine a more historical view of the heart from Noah Webster's 1828 English definition[14] of "heart," there are some differences from the modern English definitions. Webster[15] was one of the first known English language lexicographers and language reformers of his time, studying 26 languages and taking 28 years to complete the first edition of his 70,000-word dictionary. Since language changes with culture, I have included Webster's 1828 version to help bridge the gap between the current and past definitions.

Webster's 1828 Dictionary[16] gives a more robust definition that is more fitting to the biblical perspective and more closely aligned with some lexiconists of other cultures. He saw the heart as:

- The seat of affections and passions, as of love, joy, grief, enmity, courage, pleasure, etc.
- The seat of the understanding
- The seat of the will; hence, secret purposes, intentions or designs
- Person; character; used with respect to courage or kindness
- Courage; spirit; as, to take heart; to give heart; to recover heart

---

[13] Oxford Languages, in partnership with Google, state the heart as "the center of a person's thoughts and emotions, especially love, compassion, or loyalty; One's mood or feeling."

[14] MasonSoft Technology, Ltd. (2025). Heart. The American Dictionary of the English Language. https://webstersdictionary1828.com/Dictionary/heart

[15] MasonSoft Technology, Ltd. (2025). The History of Webster's Dictionary. The American Dictionary of the English Language. https://webstersdictionary1828.com/NoahWebster

[16] MasonSoft Technology, Ltd. (2025). Heart. The American Dictionary of the English Language. https://webstersdictionary1828.com/Dictionary/heart

- Secret thoughts; recesses of the mind
- Disposition of mind
- Secret meaning; real intention
- Conscience, or sense of good or ill

In summary, the more current English frameworks of the heart are more simplified than the way the heart was viewed some centuries ago, which I would attribute to natural cultural changes. Yet, philosophically, I want us to remember that God hasn't changed. The fundamental nature of God's creative design for humanity hasn't changed; thus seeking to understand our core design becomes an important pursuit because it has stood the test of time regardless of cultural change. In light of that truth, I believe we should seek universal principles that transcend changes in cultural perspectives.

My goal now is to introduce you to some more ancient cultural perspectives that have lasted over thousands of years, rather than using only the current, simplified perspective of what Google or the latest cultural perspective may say. Since the Greco-Roman culture is one of the most predominant influences on the Western civilizations of today, let's shift our focus to explore an ancient Greek perspective on the heart.

GREEK DEFINITIONS OF THE HEART

The Greek word for heart is "kardia", from which we get words like "cardiac" and "cardiology."[17] This word shows up several times in the New Testament of the Bible, and according to Thayer's Greek Lexicon,[18] this word has a fairly rich definition, referring to:

- The seat and center of all physical and spiritual life:
    - the vigor and sense of physical life
    - the center and seat of spiritual life, the soul or mind, as it is the fountain and seat of the thoughts, passions, desires, appetites, affections, purposes, endeavors (in English, we would call this the "inner man")
        - specifically, of the understanding, the faculty and seat of intelligence
        - of the will and character

[17] Abarim Publications. (2025). Kardia. https://www.abarim-publications.com/DictionaryG/k/k-a-r-d-i-a.html#

[18] Blue Letter Bible. (2025). Kardia (Strong's G2588). https://www.blueletterbible.org/lexicon/g2588/esv/mgnt/0-1/

- of the soul so far forth as it is affected and stirred in a bad way or good, or of the soul as the seat of the sensibilities, affections, emotions, desires, appetites, passions
- of a soul conscious of good or bad deeds

Please take note of how complex the view of the heart is in this Greek definition, especially when considering all of the different dynamics of what is inside of the heart. This definition implies that all sorts of diversity exist in the heart: it encompasses the soul, mind, thoughts, intelligence, emotions, passions, desires, purposes, consciousness, will, character, and more.

Similarly, James Strong's Concordance for the word "kardia" (#2588) identifies the cultural and historical background of the word:

> "In ancient Greek culture, the heart was considered the center of physical and spiritual life. This understanding was carried into the Jewish and early Christian contexts, where the heart was seen as the locus of moral and spiritual activity. The heart was believed to be the place where God communicates with humans, and where faith and understanding reside."[19]

Wow, we can gather some powerful insights from the above statements, for the focus seems to be that the heart is central to **all** of life. In essence, it is perceived that morality and spiritual activity happen in the heart, and it seems that the heart is the place where God communicates with people. From this perspective, I would liken the heart to a "garden" that is to be protected, tended, nourished, and cared for.

In light of all of this, I sense that it must be important to view the human heart appropriately and embrace how God communicates to our hearts!

There is one more cultural perspective for us to explore that can provide even deeper insight and a more holistic understanding of the human heart: the Hebraic perspective. I ask you to start taking note of the overlaps, and I ask you wrestle with your own conclusions about how you view your heart. Consider all of the other cultural perspectives by comparing and contrasting them with yours. These cultural foundations will lead us for the rest of this book, setting up what I call the "Seven Departments of the Heart."

---

[19] Bible Hub (2025-2004). 2588. Kardia. https://biblehub.com/greek/2588.htm

HEBRAIC DEFINITIONS OF THE HEART

In Hebrew, there are two versions of the word for heart, lev and levav, with both words consisting of only two letters, "lamed" (לְ) and "bet" (ב). In the ancient pictorial language script, "lamed" was drawn as a shepherd's staff and represented authority or teaching, while "bet" referred to a house or a dwelling place. The second word, levav, simply placed an emphasis on the second letter "bet," which intensified its meaning. Since Hebrew is a concrete, tangible language and not abstract like Greek and English, the two words communicated a powerful meaning:

> **lev** = "the authority of the house"
> **levav** = "the authority of the house of houses"

In simple terms, the heart is the authority, the leader, the teacher of the core parts of our lives. Metaphorically, as in a business context, I like to call the heart the "central headquarters" of a person's life. It is the place where the most important activities occur.

King Solomon, considered the wisest of the Hebrew kings, said, "Keep your heart with all vigilance, for from it flow the springs of life."[20] Another translation states that "...everything you do flows from it [the heart]."[21] King Solomon understood that life had a "central headquarters" that needed to be guarded, maintained, and preserved.

For the sake of consistency, let's take a brief look at the thoughts of some Hebrew lexiconists and examine their perspectives of the heart. We will review the thoughts of two lexicons, Brown-Driver-Briggs's Lexicon and Gesenius's Hebrew-Chaldean Lexicon.

Brown-Driver-Briggs Lexicon[22] identifies the heart as:

- Inner man, mind, will, heart
- Knowledge, thinking, reflection
- The conception of thoughts of the mind
- Imaginations of the mind

---

[20] Proverbs 4:23

[21] Proverbs 4:23 (New International Version)

[22] Blue Letter Bible (2025). לֵב. (lev). https://www.blueletterbible.org/lexicon/h3820/kjv/wlc/0-1/

- Of memory
- Inclinations, resolutions, and determinations of the will
- Conscience
- Moral character
- The seat of the appetites
- The seat of the emotions and passions
- Seat of courage

Gesenius Hebrew-Chaldee Lexicon[23] identifies the heart as:

- The seat of life
- Soul, life
- The seat of the senses, affections, and emotions of the mind
    - Examples: confidence, contempt, joy, sorrow, bitterness, fear, despair
- The mode of thinking and acting
- Character
    - Examples: prideful, pure, upright, stubborn, double-minded, sincere
- The seat of will and purpose
    - Examples: Determination, vengeance, revenge, rebellion
- Understanding, intellect, and wisdom; the faculty of thinking

CHAPTER FIVE REFLECTIVE QUESTIONS

Friends, thank you for going on this leg of the journey with me. While it did require us to take a more academic and historical approach in pursuit of learning, I believe this has been necessary to help us lay a foundation for this complex topic of the heart. As you may have noticed, the heart has many dimensions and various levels of complexity. Now that we have a common understanding regarding the various perspectives of the heart, let's take a moment and revisit some thoughts before we proceed forward.

In light of this chapter, I would like for you to review these cultural perspectives and ask yourself the following reflective questions:

1) Of the different definitions, which most grabbed your attention and why?

---

[23] Blue Letter Bible (2025). לֵב. (lev).
https://www.blueletterbible.org/lexicon/h3820/kjv/wlc/0-1/

2) Did these cultural perspectives reinforce what you already knew about the heart, or has your perspective changed?

3) Is there any perspective you disagreed with or find yourself wrestling with the concept(s)?

4) What are your questions?

5) If you were to categorize the heart into subsections, what would be on your list of five to seven subsections? For instance, as you review the definitions, if you begin seeing a theme of feelings, you could name one subsection as "Feelings." Write down your list of categories and organize the definitions according to your list.

Chapter Six

THE PURPOSES OF THE HEART

In the midst of my journey of the Lord interrupting my life, He grabbed my attention regarding the issues of my heart. It began a process of searching the scriptures for insight and to learn of the depth of what was happening inside of me. I found myself pausing to ponder King Solomon's words in Proverbs 20:5 a little further:

> **"The purpose of a man's heart is like deep water, but a man of understanding will draw it out."**

I found myself praying, "Lord, I want to be a man of understanding." I wasn't sure exactly what I was asking. I was just intrigued by the construction of this proverb. It seemed to imply that the heart was deep, like an ocean, but a person with understanding can draw out the purposes of the heart from even the deepest places. The concept initially seemed impossible, yet I can testify that the Lord has answered my prayer for understanding.

Come with me on my journey of how I meditated on this proverb.

The proverb states that the purpose, also translated as plan or counsel, of the heart is like deep water. To me, this invoked the image of an ocean that has large amounts of water, massive activity under the surface teeming with aquatic life. I imagined rolling waves, danger, depth, and an overwhelming sense of caution, given the volume of water that exponentially surpasses my existence.

Yet the scripture continued to say that "a man of understanding will draw it out."

What?! A human, with understanding, can draw out the purposes, plan, or counsel of the heart. This concept is impossible and beyond our capacity... can a human really do this?

This sparked loads of questions, so I began to ask the Lord. My meditations and questions led me to see that truly a person with the Lord's understanding has the skill, insight, and ability to draw out the deep things of the heart. Even when depth and complexity seem overwhelming, the Lord has indeed made the heart knowable for the human to understand.

I first started with studying and learning about understanding in the scripture, and I found one of my favorite scriptures in Proverbs 9:10:

> "The fear of the Lord is the beginning of wisdom, and the knowledge of the Holy One is insight (or understanding)."

This scripture gave me peace, knowing that I can know the Lord and become increasingly intimate with Him, and that He reveals insights to His friends. The imagery is like that of a significant ruler or leader who has a close friend or companion whom He trusts with precious information. Since the two are in a close relationship, the ruler has no issue with revealing his heart or intentions because he trusts his friend. In comparison, this relational concept stirred my journey in seeking the Lord about these matters and gaining His trust, which I believe is available to every believer in Jesus who seeks God as Father.

Friends, we can learn how our hearts function. We can extract the purposes, plans, and counsel that the Lord has buried deep within us. We can be a people of understanding who know how to guard and protect the thoughts and attitudes of our hearts, even as we trust and allow God to be the judge of them. We can find out what we were born for and why. We can allow the Lord to show us who we are.

Consider these scriptural thoughts to encourage us moving forward:

> King David was deemed a man **after God's heart** (1 Sam. 13:14).
>
> The Lord **weighs the heart** of humanity (Prov. 21:2).
>
> King David prayed and said, **"Know my heart"** (Ps. 139:23).
>
> Jeremiah stated that God can **give us a heart to know Him** (Jer. 24:7).
>
> The Lord **looks at and judges the heart** of humanity (1 Sam. 16:7; Heb. 4:12).

Metaphorically, consider the idea of us putting on scuba diving equipment or using a submarine to explore the deep waters of our hearts. May the Lord help us to see what we can't naturally see. May He reveal the beauty and the capacity of who we are. May He show us that He alone can make us so amazing, for we are fearfully and wonderfully made in His image. May praise come off our lips as we discover what only He can show us.

CHAPTER SIX LISTENING PRAYER QUESTIONS

1) Lord, what do You want to say to me regarding this chapter?

2) Lord, am I ready to go on this journey with You?

3) Lord, is there anything holding me back from going forward with You on this journey?

4) Lord, what else to You want to say? Or, what else do I need to know about the purposes of my heart?

AUTHOR'S NOTE

The next chapters of this book are intended to help you draw out the counsel, purposes, and plans of your heart. I want to provide a learning environment that helps conceptualize the heart, articulate its function, and outline the seven departments of the heart in a way that makes it more understandable. Remember, we are about to plunge into deep waters, and I want to make sure you have the appropriate scuba gear on for the journey. My hope is for you to become a person of understanding who can draw out the purposes of your heart.[24]

[24] As a reminder, my hope is based on Proverbs 20:5, which reads, "The purpose in a man's heart is like deep water, but a man of understanding will draw it out." I believe that each one of us, with training and proper engagement with the Lord, can be a person of understanding.

Chapter Seven

FUNCTIONS OF THE HEART

The human heart is the central headquarters of every human's life. According to God's design, it was intended to be responsive and sensitive to God, yet it was marred by sin. Praise God for being the One to fix our heart issues by giving us a heart transplant and granting us the grace to have the opportunity to learn of God's original intention. He knows how to help each of us reconnect back to Him according to His will. Let's learn together about how to guard, keep, protect, and govern our hearts according to His design.

Even though each person will govern his or her heart differently, there are some consistent core principles that all of us can consider regarding how the heart functions. We all can learn to let God be the leader, manager, commander-in-chief, president, chief executive officer, lawgiver, and judge of our hearts. However, if we don't know how the heart functions, we can miss out on guarding, keeping, protecting, and caring for the most precious thing that God has given us as believers in Jesus: a fresh new start on life with a new heart.

Let's first start our discussion with three ideologies regarding the function of the heart. These are the basics, the attributes, and the leadership of the heart. I'll offer some minimal commentary, yet I'll encourage you to ponder the scriptures I list as a way to process more of the concepts on your own. This chapter will set up our final discussions on the specific departments of the heart.

THE BASICS OF THE HEART

1) The heart needs to be replaced with a **new, viable, God-receptive heart.**

"I will give them an undivided heart and put a new spirit in them; I will remove from them their heart of stone and give them a heart of flesh" (Ezekiel 11:19, NIV).

God has to supernaturally give each of us a new heart that is receptive to Him in order for heart change to become possible. God's gift of salvation, given because of the work of Jesus Christ, is like the new heart that is given to a heart transplant patient. Once the new heart is available, new life can come to the patient. God performs the surgery by removing the old and giving us the new.

2) The heart is the **headquarters of your life**; everything comes out of it.

"Above all else, guard your heart, for everything you do flows from it" (Proverbs 4:23, NIV).

When I say "headquarters," this refers to a metaphorical image of a major business corporation's main office, which oversees the affairs of the entire organization. The headquarters usually houses the primary administrative and managerial staff, and it is the place where most overarching strategic planning, decision-making, and training happens. The headquarters are divided into unique interdependent departments that work together to fulfill the organizational mission and vision. Additionally, headquarters will typically house the offices of the most powerful individuals, including the president, chief vice presidents, and other prominent figures who significantly influence the corporation's affairs.

I liken the human heart to this metaphor of headquarters because it can be used to learn the affairs of our hearts through the help of Holy Spirit. Each heart department serves a variety of purposes. While we will discuss these departments in greater detail in the next section of the book, I am now introducing them briefly in order to help you better connect with the headquarters metaphor. The Department of Intellect is where our meditations and thoughts operate, while the Department of Emotions and Feelings is where we are moved to respond to life depending on what we feel in a given moment. The Department of Passions points to areas of our calling, and the Department of Desires identifies deep yearnings that are best satisfied by God. Our Department of Conscience checks us and keeps us in line with God's intentions, our Department of Character is the expression of the affairs of our hearts, while our Department of Will is the place of decision-making. All of the departments work interdependently.

3) The heart is **deep and complex.**

"The purpose in a man's heart is like deep water, but a man of understanding will draw it out" (Proverbs 20:5).

The heart is difficult to understand. Again, consider the heart like a deep ocean with different types of wave currents, various levels of water pressure, dangerous conditions, and diversities of marine life. That's a lot of complexity! The volume and depth of what the heart experiences is too great for our human understanding; thus, we need God's perspective, wisdom, and insights about how to navigate the heart. May God help us become a people of understanding to draw out the depths of the heart.

4) The heart needs to be **regularly tested, judged, and examined.**

> "For the word of God is living and active, sharper than any two-edged sword, piercing to the division of soul and of spirit, of joints and of marrow, and discerning the thoughts and intentions of the heart" (Hebrews 4:12).

One of the most challenging maintenance factors of the heart is to allow God to regularly test, judge, examine, and search our hearts. We tend to self-examine and self-judge our own hearts according to our cultural standards, yet we fail to let God, our Maker, truly show us what is happening inside of us. I personally know this challenge, for it can be scary, tedious, and humbling to go before God to let Him show me what's happening inside of me. To live, remain, and regulate our peace with God, it is essential to let Him examine our hearts.

THE ATTRIBUTES OF THE HEART

5) The heart shows a person's **real character.**

> "...the Lord said to Samuel, 'Do not look on his appearance or on the height of his stature...For the Lord sees not as man sees: man looks on the outward appearance, but the Lord looks on the heart" (1 Samuel 16:7).

God's great prophet Samuel was graced with the privilege to anoint the first kings of Israel. At the ceremony to anoint one of the sons of Jesse as king, the prophet was originally influenced by societal constructs and expectations, which would have dictated that the oldest son be selected as king. However, God taught Samuel that He does not look at the outward appearance of a person like humans do, but God looks at the heart, where the true character lives. It happened to be the youngest of Jesse's eight sons, David, who would be the chosen king, and be a man after God's heart.[25] The real character of a person is buried in the heart.

6) The heart is where **evil things originate.**

"For from within, out of the heart of man, come evil thoughts, sexual immorality, theft, murder, adultery, coveting, wickedness, deceit, sensuality, envy, slander, pride, foolishness. All these evil things come from within, and they defile a person" (Mark 7:21-23).

In order to deal with the evil things within, a change of heart must be the focus rather than mere behavior modifications. Often, some cultures expect a person to simply change their behaviors and demonstrate good morality rather than attempting to challenge that person toward a heart change. Everything comes from the heart, whether positive or negative, good or bad, righteous or unrighteous; it's all in and from the heart. So, if a person wants real transformation, a genuine change of heart is essential.

7) The heart is the place of our **thinking and meditations.**

"The Lord saw that the wickedness of man was great in the earth, and that every intention of the thoughts of his heart was only evil continually" (Genesis 6:5).

"Let the words of my mouth and the meditation of my heart be acceptable in your sight, O Lord, my rock and my redeemer" (Psalm 19:14).

In various cultural contexts, a person's thoughts and meditations are attributed to the mind or the brain. Biblically, however, thinking and meditation are connected to the heart. I believe that when we think or behave in righteous or evil ways, it is a heart issue, rather than a head, mind, or brain issue. To have a whole heart before the Lord, we must consider that our thinking and meditation are attributes of the heart rather than a simple faculty of the mind, brain, or head. How we think and meditate on the Lord affects our lives.

8) The heart is **like soil,** for it receives seed and produces fruit.

"When anyone hears the word of the kingdom and does not understand it, the evil one comes and snatches away what has been

[25] 1 Samuel 13:14

sown in his heart...As for what was sown on good soil, this is the one who hears the word and understands it. He indeed bears fruit and yields, in one case a hundredfold, in another sixty, and in another thirty" (Matt. 13:19a; 23).

The heart was originally intended to be receptive to God's communication with humanity, yet sin separated the relationship. The unredeemed heart was a heart of stone that could not be fruitful. Yet, through the work of Jesus, each human is given the opportunity to understand and garden the soil of their heart for fruitfulness. In other words, God had to perform a supernatural work of replacing the original heart and giving us a God-responsive new heart. We now have the ability to embark on a journey of living according to God's original design, where God plants seeds within our hearts, cares for us, and produces fruitfulness from us.

THE LEADERSHIP OF THE HEART

Since the human heart can be likened to soil and to the central headquarters of an organization, we can draw on principles from both gardening and leadership to consider how to lead the heart. Ultimately, the heart is most tender to its Creator God and is led best by His words. Also, the heart is designed to be pursued, provided for, and protected. God best leads the human heart in partnership with people of authority in the life of an individual. Whether we recognize it or not, we are all led by our hearts.

9) The Word of God must be the **chief gardener** of the human heart.

"For the word of God is living and active, sharper than any two-edged sword, piercing to the division of soul and of spirit, of joints and of marrow, and discerning the thoughts and intentions of the heart" (Heb. 4:12).

We naturally allow many other voices to guide our affairs, sometimes without even being aware of it. The voices we listen to can come from evil spirits or people who have an agenda. We must become aware of who we listen to and continually turn from those other voices to seek God's voice through His Word instead, by continually submitting to Him as the chief gardener of our hearts. God wants to be the chief gardener because He loves us and knows that His nurturing is what will allow us to thrive and come back into alignment with His original design. He alone knows the depth of who we are and the intentions of our hearts. No one else has the full rights to teach, lead, guide, judge, examine, and search our hearts the way God does.

10) The heart **needs to be directed.**

"The king's heart is a stream of water in the hand of the Lord; he turns it wherever he will" (Proverbs 21:1).

"May the Lord direct your hearts to the love of God and to the steadfastness of Christ" (2 Thessalonians 3:5).

The Greek word for "direct" in 2 Thessalonians 3 is "kateuthunó." The word refers to making a straight path without obstacles. More specifically, this word

> "...evokes the act of straightening or directing a path so that movement toward a destination becomes unhindered. In Scripture the verb consistently presents God as the One who removes obstacles, aligns purposes, and sets the course for His people. The picture is that of a royal road being graded and leveled so the king may pass; spiritually, the King Himself clears the way for His servants and also aligns their hearts toward His will."[26]

If we consider this connotation, God wants to make a straight, obstacle-free, purposeful path for our hearts toward Him and His will.

11) The heart **can be pursued.**

"But now your kingdom will not endure; the Lord has sought out a man after his own heart and appointed him ruler of his people, because you have not kept the Lord's command..." (1 Sam. 13:14, NIV).

"After removing Saul, he made David their king. God testified concerning him: 'I have found David son of Jesse, a man after my own heart; he will do everything I want him to do" (Acts 13:22, NIV).

I believe that since God, as Creator, gave humans the ability to pursue His heart, humans can also pursue the hearts of one another. Yet, I

---

[26] https://biblehub.com/greek/2720.htm

believe this takes skill and training. As I'm about to outline in the next section of this book, there are different departments of the heart that operate certain ways. The Lord pursues all of our hearts uniquely, and in turn, we can pursue His and other people's hearts as we understand how the heart operates. I believe the wisdom and understanding from the Lord, through relationship with Holy Spirit, helps us pursue the heart of another.

12) The human heart **should be guarded vigilantly.**

"Above all else, guard your heart..." (Prov. 4:23a, NIV).

Most major organizations around the world have their headquarters guarded under significant security as well as comprehensive governance policies. The security measures may include heavily monitored premises with cameras viewing all aspects of the headquarters. There may be cybersecurity tests and monitoring to make sure there isn't a breach in privacy. In addition, the organization may have layers of policies written to establish an order of operations, navigate conflicts, and bind people to a code of conduct. The goal is for this complex, delicate system to be protected against violations that could threaten the company.

We must guard our hearts from all sorts of attacks, for these attacks can destroy our lives. All throughout scripture, the Lord has given us indicators, clues, frameworks, governance, and practical applications on how to train, lead, guard, and protect our hearts. Our hearts are our central headquarters; it is critical that we do not minimize the importance of protecting it.

CHAPTER SEVEN LISTENING PRAYER QUESTIONS

1) Lord, what do You want to say about the functions of my heart?

2) Lord, what part of this chapter do You want me to focus on?

3) Lord, will You clarify those areas of this chapter that I don't understand or parts that are challenging me?

4) Lord, what else do You want to say about this chapter?

Chapter Eight

THE DEPARTMENTS OF THE HEART

From my study of scripture, I have discerned seven departments that make up the heart. I came to this conclusion by taking the Hebrew words for heart "lev" and "levav", along with the Greek word "kardia", and I traced them all throughout scripture. With each passage, I examined the context and created organized categories, which I now call heart departments. For my purposes, I only acknowledge seven, yet as you study more, you may want to classify additional departments.

Here are my seven heart departments that make up the central headquarters of our lives:

1. The Department of Intellect
2. The Department of Emotions and Feelings
3. The Department of Passions
4. The Department of Desires
5. The Department of Conscience
6. The Department of Character
7. The Department of Will

As we get started, I want to share with you what I sensed that Holy Spirit shared with me during a time of listening prayer.

I asked the Lord: *"What are You saying about my heart?"*

Here is what I sensed the Lord communicated:

> **"Train your mind.**
> **Lead your emotions and feelings.**
> **Fully give yourself to your passions.**
> **Allow Me to fulfill your desires.**
> **Don't dishonor your conscience.**
> **Walk in the fullness of character.**
> **Decide toward the things of God. May My will be done."**

As I pondered these statements, I began to see the practical applications for each department. I need to give you this practical framework first to lay a foundation before we get into the technicalities of how these departments function interdependently. Our Father wants to communicate with us because He desires for us to live with a pure, integrated, and whole heart rather than a disjointed, compartmentalized, and disunified heart. God knows that when our hearts are unified, we can then access the full power and capacity He's provided and put within us to allow us to accomplish all that He has for us on the planet.

As we transition into more details of the heart departments, let us first look at a few examples of a whole heart and a pure heart in the Bible:

SCRIPTURAL EXAMPLES RELATED TO A WHOLE HEART:

Example 1: King David charges his son Solomon to have a whole heart when he becomes the new king.

> "And you, Solomon my son, know the God of your father and serve him with a **whole heart** and with a willing mind [in Hebrew, the word for "mind" is actually "soul"], for the Lord searches all hearts and understands every plan and thought. If you seek him, he will be found by you, but if you forsake him, he will cast you off forever" (1 Chronicles 28:9).

Example 2: One of the kings of Judah, King Amaziah, does right in the Lord's eyes, yet Amaziah still compromised his allegiance to worshipping the Lord alone.

> "And he did what was right in the eyes of the Lord, yet not with a **whole heart**. And as soon as the royal power was firmly his, he killed his servants who had struck down the king his father (2 Chronicles 25:2-3)...After Amaziah came from striking down the Edomites, he brought the gods of the men of Seir and set them up as his gods and worshiped them, making offerings to them. Therefore the Lord was angry with Amaziah..." (2 Chronicles 25:14-15a).

Example 3: God gives promises to Israel, and He identifies how Israel will return to Him.

> "I will give them a heart to know me, that I am the Lord, and they shall be my people and I will be their God, for they shall return to me with their **whole heart**" (Jeremiah 24:7).

SCRIPTURAL EXAMPLES OF A PURE HEART:

Example 1: The Psalmist identifies those types of people who will be near to the Lord.

> "Who shall ascend the hill of the Lord? And who shall stand in his holy place? He who has clean hands and a **pure heart**, who does not lift up his soul to what is false and does not swear deceitfully" (Psalms 24:3-4).

Example 2: Jesus' Sermon on the Mount includes a beatitude that promises that those who are pure in heart will be blessed a certain way.

> "Blessed are the **pure in heart**, for they shall see God" (Matthew 5:8).

Example 3: The Apostle Paul tells his spiritual son how love comes from a pure heart.

> "The aim of our charge is love that issues from a **pure heart** and a good conscience and a sincere faith" (1 Timothy 1:5).

Please continue with me on the quest of learning how to integrate, purify, and live with a whole heart. My goal is to identify the individual components of the heart from what I have gathered from scripture, and then offer you questions to ask the Lord for further insights. This quest challenges our frameworks of what's really happening inside of our hearts and will lead us to learn from our Maker. I don't claim to have all the knowledge or answers about each department, but I will provide an overview of what each department encompasses, an anecdote from my own journey of understanding it, some scriptures to consider, and more listening prayer questions to start your conversation with the Lord.

While you have already been exercising listening prayer, the next few sections will take us a little deeper in our understanding. As a reminder, in Psalm 139:17-18 (NIV), King David prays to God about how precious and vast are the thoughts of God. David wanted the thoughts of God:

> "How precious to me are your thoughts, God! How vast is the sum of them! Were I to count them, they would outnumber the grains of sand..."

Therefore, when we pray, let's consider that God has a lot to say to us if we are willing to embrace His thoughts about us. He has enough words to overhaul all our pride-filled traditions and frameworks that give us a false sense of security. We can ask God to reveal His thoughts that speak so specifically to the core places of our hearts. Our God has thoughts that will shatter lies, reveal purpose, and transform your life. Let Him speak to you.

As we continue our listening prayer, remember to write down the question, ask Holy Spirit to speak to you, and write down those things that come to you in words, pictures, whole phrases, or hunches.

At this stage, just write what comes to mind, and later evaluate them within a safe community and through the word of God. God knows how to communicate with you in your way.

CHAPTER EIGHT LISTENING PRAYER QUESTIONS

1) Lord, what are You saying to me about my heart?

2) Lord, what parts of my heart are not whole?

3) Lord, what parts of my heart are impure?

4) Lord, what do You want me to know about fractured parts of my heart?

5) Lord, what do You want me to know about the things that cause impurities in my heart?

6) Lord, what else do You want me to know?

Chapter Nine

THE DEPARTMENT OF INTELLECT

"Train Your Mind"

WHAT'S INSIDE THE DEPARTMENT OF INTELLECT?

- Cognition
- Memory
- Internal Dialogue
- Words
- Understanding
- Reflections
- Meditations
- Speaking
- Thinking

OVERVIEW OF THE DEPARTMENT

I want to start our discussion with the Department of Intellect because it is probably the most developed part of the heart, especially in the western world. For most of us western-educated learners, this department is what we call "the mind." However, using a Hebraic biblical framework, I believe the mind is best situated in the heart since numerous scriptures point to thinking, meditating, and speaking happening within and from the heart. For my purposes, I will continue to use the term "mind" since it's familiar in many cultures, but I will situate the mind as one of the heart's departments. This department, I believe, is like the front door into and out of the heart.[27]

I use the metaphor of the front door because one theme of scripture is that God's words are the foundation of the human lifestyle. In essence, when people open their hearts and meditate, hide, heed, remember, study, and live by God's word, it affects their whole life. Everything in their heart has the potential to change[28] if they allow God's process.

[27] Matthew 12:34; Matthew 15:18-19; Mark 7:21; Luke 6:45

[28] Romans 8:5-8; Romans 12:2; Colossians 3:2

Intellection is our ability to know, acquire information, think, use language, and process internally. It is the foundation for reasoning, cognitive processing, dialogue, meditations, and memory. It's trained by our cultural and educational experiences, our family's traditions and patterns, and our internal dialogues about how we think about ourselves and others. Yet our intellect is trained best by the Lord's words. He wants us to embrace what He says about life in general, about us specifically, and about His perspective of others.

To receive optimal functionality out of this department, we need to remove places of pride, lies, and traditions that hinder us from knowing the Lord. Holy Spirit is the best manager of this department because He knows how to teach us about God, lead us to truth, and remind us of what Jesus says to us.[29] Our job is to humble ourselves before Holy Spirit and submit to the Word of God. We continually need to resist pride, speak truth to lies, and create disciplines that are centered on God's way.

PRACTICAL STORY

Growing up, my intellect was formed by my cultural context, which included parents who emphasized the importance of doing well and completing the formal educational system of the United States. My parents expected us to complete the requirements of the system with perfect marks. We were praised when we received top grades and awards, yet challenged to do better or punished if there were anything less. Based on this context, my perception was that if I earned a B grade in any course, it was as if I had failed. Our educational focus was not on how we felt about school, or our likes or dislikes, or our calling in life; it was about earning good grades, pursuing chemistry as a college major, and securing a job that makes us enough money to live.

My experiences created my intellectual capacity and developed a strong focus on my cognition, intellectualism, knowledge retention, and short and long-term memory. Other aspects of my heart needed training, but they remained underdeveloped because of the emphasis on this one Department of Intellect. This caused divisive breaks in my other heart departments. This mindset was further reinforced outside of my family, when I heard popular culture say phrases like:

- "There is an 18-inch gap between your head and your heart."

---

[29] John 14:26; John 16:13; 1 John 2:27

- "This is not a heart issue, but a head issue. Use your common sense."
- "Tell me what you think, but I don't want to hear about your feelings."

The above statements implied that my intellect was superior to everything else and that I should be separated from other areas of my heart. It subtly dishonored my emotions and feelings, and I inferred that they should not even be discussed. In fact, there were times when I was considered weak if I communicated certain emotions. As a result of my cultural experiences, I trained myself to set aside my emotions and give the correct, culturally acceptable intellectual responses.

My experiences led me to a place where I did not understand how to express or articulate my emotions, passions, or desires in a healthy way. I had emotions and feelings, but never truly received comfort for them or led them well. I minimized my passions and desires, especially when they conflicted with what my intellectual capacity communicated was best for me. Even in choosing chemistry as my field of study in college, I reduced my desires and passions to merely appreciating the basic benefits and hopeful rewards attached to the degree I chose, despite it not being my true calling. My intellect could have enhanced my understanding of my emotions, feelings, desires, and passions, and the like. Yet, I was challenged to spend years subordinating everything to the altar of the "high and mighty intellect" or, put more simply, my mind. My experiences invoked pride, lies, and traditions, which affected my relationships, masked my insecurities, and led me to callous and numb important parts of my heart. Again, my mind was exalted, praised, and honored, while no other department was given as much attention.

As I grew in my relationship with the Lord and learned about the wholeness that God wanted for me, I came to realize the power of integrating my intellect with all other departments of my heart. It has brought such sweet communion with God and others in my life. My intellect has helped me grow from the immature 15-year-old boy I was inside to someone who can integrate all of my heart departments. I wanted a pure heart that could see God (Matthew 5:8) and a whole heart devoted to the Lord. I chose to let the word of God, which alone has the capacity to integrate the heart, be the object of my thoughts and meditations. The training keeps me disciplined in reading the scriptures, monitoring my thoughts, discerning truth from lies, and doing the hard work of renewing my patterns in all areas of my heart. The journey has enhanced my emotions, led me to my passions, redirected my desires, developed my character, sensitized my conscience, and clarified God's will for my life.

This journey has been well worth it!

SCRIPTURAL MEDITATIONS FOR THE DEPARTMENT OF THE INTELLECT

The Lord saw that the wickedness of man was great in the earth, and that **every intention of the thoughts of his heart** was only evil continually... (Genesis 6:5).

Hannah was **praying in her heart**, and her lips were moving but her voice was not heard (1 Samuel 1:13, NIV).

May these words of my mouth and this **meditation of my heart** be pleasing in your sight, Lord, my Rock and my Redeemer (Psalms 19:14, NIV).

Knowing their thoughts, Jesus said, “Why do you entertain **evil thoughts in your hearts**?” (Matthew 9:4, NIV).

Immediately Jesus knew in his spirit that this was what they were **thinking in their hearts**, and he said to them, “Why are you thinking these things?” (Mark 2:8, NIV).

CHAPTER NINE LISTENING PRAYER QUESTIONS

1) Lord, what do I need to know about my Department of Intellect?
2) Lord, who or what has regularly trained my Department of Intellect?
3) Lord, will You reveal to me what I regularly meditate on in my heart?
4) Lord, what are some lies that I am believing?
5) Lord, what is the truth instead of the lies I’m believing?
6) Lord, what practical changes do I need to make regarding my Department of Intellect?

Chapter Ten

THE DEPARTMENT OF EMOTIONS AND FEELINGS
"Lead your Emotions"

WHAT'S INSIDE THE DEPARTMENT OF EMOTIONS AND FEELINGS?

- Discernment
- Emotions
- Burdens
- Feelings
- Hunches
- Intuition
- Senses
- Spirituality

OVERVIEW OF THE DEPARTMENT

Emotions and feelings are complex to articulate, especially in cultures where they are dismissed or deemed unimportant. What I mean is that emotions and feelings are important and beautiful communicators, but if they are not valued, they can create a disjointed and dysregulated heart. We were all created to be emotional beings with feelings, but depending on our cultural training, such as family, church communities, and schooling, our expression and understanding of them will have different ranges. For instance, consider a pastor of a church community who may feel shame about recurring sin they want to overcome. Instead of openly confessing their sin and seeking help, they live in shame and never disclose their challenges to anyone on the team for the fear of losing their job or credibility as a minister. One reason is that the church's culture projects the idea that people should lead tidy, sin-free, polished lives; it implies that there is no safe place to struggle with sin. Therefore, deep shame becomes normative within that person's heart, and they may either never overcome it, or they may feel forced to seek help outside of the church.

Our cultures teach us so many things about how we are to emote or feel about life, yet these beautiful communicators are meant to help us live life fully. Emotions are designed to move us along in life. Consider how sadness can give us an outlet for releasing our grief, so that we don't get stuck in a state of emotional paralysis or numbness. Alternatively, ponder on how healthy expressions of fear keep us within acceptable boundaries or away from danger. Feelings grant us great pleasure in life, such as the refreshing feeling of drinking water when thirsty or the relaxed feeling of sitting down after standing for a long period of time. We experience emotions and feelings all the time, and they move us to act.

As we continue forward, I have a question for us to process:

What would happen if we trained our emotions and feelings more regularly and examined this part of our lives routinely?

This next anecdote will hopefully help us consider the necessity of learning, training, and leading our emotions and feelings.

PRACTICAL STORY

Earlier in the book, I mentioned that I was challenged by a mentor because I responded to a situation as if I were a 15-year-old boy, even though I was in my late thirties. The core issue was that my maturity level was the result of never training my emotions to function according to their design. I'd had emotional experiences as a young person, but without training, I covered, masked, and medicated away those intense feelings and emotions and never led them to health. In other words, my emotions and feelings were indicators of something happening inside of me, but I did not know how to examine them properly in order to lead them.

As a metaphorical example, imagine our emotions and feelings are like indicator lights on a car dashboard to identify the need for an oil change, check the engine, evaluate low tire pressure, or warn us of low fuel. All of these lights identify something specific, yet there needs to be an examination of what exactly is happening. As the driver, we have some choices to make. One choice is to immediately panic and stop the car when the indicator lights turn on. Another choice is to notice the light and research the owner's manual to learn what the light means. Additionally, we can choose to schedule an appointment and take the vehicle to get examined by a professional mechanic, or we can choose to do the work on our own. Regardless of the choices we make, we have to make a decision about our willingness to pay the price to deal with whatever is happening with the car.

Several years ago, we bought a used car that had its "check engine" light come on some time after we bought it. I took the car to the dealership maintenance team, and they told me it would be a multiple thousand dollar fix. I had only bought the car for $3500. I had to judge if it was worth it for me to fix this big engine problem. I asked the mechanic questions about the drivability of the car, and he said that it could have certain problems. Based on his professional advice, I decided not to fix the car and drove it for the next four years with the check engine light remaining on, with no major problems with the car.

In another situation, I bought a car with a Tire Pressure Monitoring System (TPMS) light that kept coming on. I got it examined and decided to complete the work for under $200.

In light of these car examples, taking care of a vehicle can be costly, inconvenient, and time-consuming; similarly, our emotions and feelings can be costly, inconvenient, and time-consuming. If my "check engine" light is on in my health, showing itself as feelings of grogginess, lethargy, and sluggishness, I will have to make some decisions to get it examined by a health professional and/or seek the Lord about what's happening within me. Once I get clarity on what's happening, I have to make more decisions about counting the cost of maintaining that part of my lifestyle based on the diagnosis. If the cost is a diet change, I must count the cost to maintain it. If the cost is medication to regulate certain biochemical levels of the body, I have to maintain that. Or, if the cost is to reorient other lifestyle decisions to lessen my stress levels, I need to maintain it. Regardless of the diagnosis, there will be a cost.

It is important to take care of this department by allowing the indicator lights of emotions and feelings to illuminate and then being willing to examine them. If we are not used to doing this, it will feel awkward at first, but it will begin to improve our emotional health. If we just shut off or dismiss our emotions and feelings without examination, we will cause damage to our lives through our choice to ignore. We might even try to medicate or alter our emotions, or to knowingly allow unhealthy emotions or feelings to remain active. Those emotions and feelings will become toxic, rusted, gunky, numb, dangerous, or any mixture of these.

SCRIPTURAL MEDITATIONS FOR THE DEPARTMENT OF EMOTIONS AND FEELINGS

In the following scriptures, read **slowly** and consider the emotions and feelings present in each situation.

In the first story, the people of Israel had just lost their beloved prophetic sister, Miriam, Moses' big sister. The people were thirsty, likely scared, antagonistic, and probably were experiencing a plethora of other emotions. The emotional climate seemed quite high for everyone, including leadership.

> And the people of Israel, the whole congregation, came into the wilderness of Zin in the first month, and the people stayed in Kadesh. And Miriam died there and was buried there. Now there was no water for the congregation. And they assembled themselves together against Moses and against Aaron. And the people quarreled with Moses and said, "Would that we had perished when our brothers perished before the Lord! Why have you brought the assembly of the Lord into this wilderness, that we should die here, both we and our cattle? And why have you made us come up out of Egypt to bring us to this evil place? It is no place for grain or figs or vines or pomegranates, and there is no water to drink." Then Moses and Aaron went from the presence of the assembly to the entrance of the tent of meeting and fell on their faces. And the glory of the Lord appeared to them, and the Lord spoke to Moses, saying, "Take the staff, and assemble the congregation, you and Aaron your brother, and tell the rock before their eyes to yield its water. So you shall bring water out of the rock for them and give drink to the congregation and their cattle." And Moses took the staff from before the Lord, as he commanded him.
>
> Then Moses and Aaron gathered the assembly together before the rock, and he said to them, "Hear now, you rebels: shall we bring water for you out of this rock?" And Moses lifted up his hand and struck the rock with his staff twice, and water came out abundantly, and the congregation drank, and their livestock. And the Lord said to Moses and Aaron, "Because you did not believe in me, to uphold me as holy in the eyes of the people of Israel, therefore you shall not bring this assembly into the land that I have given them." These are the waters of Meribah, where the people of Israel quarreled with the Lord, and through them he showed himself holy (Numbers 20:1-13).

The Lord told Moses to speak to the rock, yet instead Moses struck the rock twice. Consider what Moses must have felt that caused him to choose to strike the rock. Think about how he might have felt when he recognized he lost the opportunity to see the promised land.

For the next story, I invite you to consider the emotions and feelings present between a Philistine woman named Delilah and one of God's chosen judges of Israel named Samson.

> After this he loved a woman in the Valley of Sorek, whose name was Delilah. And the lords of the Philistines came up to her and said to her, "Seduce him, and see where his great strength lies, and by what means we may overpower him, that we may bind him to humble him. And we will each give you 1,100 pieces of silver." So Delilah said to Samson, "Please tell me where your great strength lies, and how you might be bound, that one could subdue you."
>
> Samson said to her, "If they bind me with seven fresh bowstrings that have not been dried, then I shall become weak and be like any other man." Then the lords of the Philistines brought up to her seven fresh bowstrings that had not been dried, and she bound him with them. Now she had men lying in ambush in an inner chamber. And she said to him, "The Philistines are upon you, Samson!" But he snapped the bowstrings, as a thread of flax snaps when it touches the fire. So the secret of his strength was not known.
>
> Then Delilah said to Samson, "Behold, you have mocked me and told me lies. Please tell me how you might be bound." And he said to her, "If they bind me with new ropes that have not been used, then I shall become weak and be like any other man." So Delilah took new ropes and bound him with them and said to him, "The Philistines are upon you, Samson!" And the men lying in ambush were in an inner chamber. But he snapped the ropes off his arms like a thread.
>
> Then Delilah said to Samson, "Until now you have mocked me and told me lies. Tell me how you might be bound." And he said to her, "If you weave the seven locks of my head with the web and fasten it tight with the pin, then I shall become weak and be like any other man." So while he slept, Delilah took the seven locks of his head and wove them into the web. And she made them tight with the pin and said to him, "The Philistines are upon you, Samson!" But he awoke from his sleep and pulled away the pin, the loom, and the web.

> And she said to him, "How can you say, 'I love you,' when your heart is not with me? You have mocked me these three times, and you have not told me where your great strength lies." And when she pressed him hard with her words day after day, and urged him, his soul was vexed to death. And he told her all his heart, and said to her, "A razor has never come upon my head, for I have been a Nazirite to God from my mother's womb. If my head is shaved, then my strength will leave me, and I shall become weak and be like any other man."
>
> When Delilah saw that he had told her all his heart, she sent and called the lords of the Philistines, saying, "Come up again, for he has told me all his heart." Then the lords of the Philistines came up to her and brought the money in their hands. She made him sleep on her knees. And she called a man and had him shave off the seven locks of his head. Then she began to torment him, and his strength left him. And she said, "The Philistines are upon you, Samson!" And he awoke from his sleep and said, "I will go out as at other times and shake myself free." But he did not know that the Lord had left him. And the Philistines seized him and gouged out his eyes and brought him down to Gaza and bound him with bronze shackles. And he ground at the mill in the prison. But the hair of his head began to grow again after it had been shaved (Judges 16:4-22).

Delilah's manipulative attempts stirred Samson's emotions, leading him to reveal information that consequently cost him his strength and left him bound, with his eyes plucked out, reduced to a servant of his enemies.

CHAPTER TEN LISTENING PRAYER QUESTIONS

1) Lord, what do You need me to know about my emotions and feelings?
2) Lord, which emotions tend to lead my life regularly?
3) Lord, which of my emotions do You want to heal?
4) Lord, will You show me how You want to lead my emotions?
5) What more do You want me to know about my emotions?

Chapter Eleven

THE DEPARTMENT OF PASSIONS
"Fully Give Yourself to Your Passions"

WHAT'S INSIDE THE DEPARTMENT OF PASSIONS?

- Suffering
- Afflictions
- Calling
- Disciplines
- Enduring Pain
- Hardships
- Motivations
- Drive
- Perseverance

OVERVIEW OF THE DEPARTMENT

One of the Greek words for passions is the word pathos, referring to a powerful inner impulse that dominates and potentially overrides the will. This inner impulse is so powerful that an individual will even suffer for the sake of it. The emotional drive behind this passion motivates a person to give themselves over to the specific passion. A few related concepts to passion are zeal, ardor, and jealousy. For instance, if one is zealous, he or she has such a strong impulse to fulfill a specific mission. If jealous, a person can get to the point of taking someone's life. Passion, along with its counterparts, carries inside the human heart a prompting so powerful that it is difficult to stop because of its drive a goal.

This is the heart department where one's calling lies. If you examine your passions well, you will find the places in your life that you are willing to give yourself to fully at any and all costs. Your passion could be for some sort of cause related to your culture. It could also be for some sort of change in your family line, such as changing some unrighteous patterned behavior that repeats itself within the family. One indicator of passion is that you become fixated on a matter, and you are willing to endure whatever circumstance may come in order to grasp the passion of your heart. For instance, in John 12, Jesus' passion was to be a sinless sacrifice to restore humanity's relationship back to God, and so Jesus fully obeyed God. Jesus said, "For I have not spoken on my own authority, but the Father who sent me has himself given me a commandment—what to say and what to speak. And I know that his commandment is eternal life. What I say, therefore, I say as the Father has told me" (John 12:49-50). Jesus gave His life over to full obedience to God, demonstrating His passion and willingness to suffer at all costs for the agenda of God on the earth.

PRACTICAL STORY

I have a passion for my family to be whole and healthy.

Both of my parents experienced hardship in their early years of life. My paternal grandmother died when my father was seven years old, and my dad watched my grandfather take care of three boys by himself even in the midst of his grief. My maternal grandmother never married, having six kids by two men who never chose to marry her. My mother watched my grandmother endure emotional abuse as she attempted to care for her children. My maternal grandfather had nine known children with five different mothers, only one of which he ever married. As a grandchild of these grandparents, I watched my father's passion to stay faithful to us as a family even through his own personal challenges of loss and heartbreak. I also watched my mother overcome her own emotional challenges and endure through hardships. My parents suffered and remained faithful in their lives in their own way due in large part to the example of perseverance my grandparents had modeled for them. I live in this legacy.

I am passionate about my children's development and training, protectively praying, preaching, and teaching them about healthy family. I am also passionate about my marriage because my wife is God's gift to me, a gift to my children, and a gift to our community. Our marriage provides emotional and spiritual stability to my children and the people in our community. This passion evokes my emotions at levels where I find myself angry at systems, frameworks, and distractions that want to steal from my marriage, my children, and my community. I've learned that unrighteous systems, frameworks, and distractions are built by demonic spirits and their human partners who choose to partner with these spirits. As I have recognized more about my passions, it has confirmed why courageous boldness rises up in me to build things that bring change. I passionately want God's kingdom to come, such as His systems, His structures, and His authority, on earth as it is in heaven. I want to build things that honor the Lord's order and not sinful human experience.

The Lord uses my faith, my family, and His revelations to fuel and reinforce my passions. My faith in the Lord informs the areas where my passion lies. The Lord gripped my life when I was a young 18-year-old college student and set a fire within me to be a generational change agent. I have seen with my own eyes my brother and sister to come to know the Lord, and I have watched years of transformation in my parents. My family story is something I inherited and learned about from a young age, for my dad and mom would tell me stories of both life-giving and broken areas of the family. I would store these stories in my heart to fuel changes needed in the family line. This passion leads me to tell my children stories of change, defeat, and victory in the family quite often. In addition, God's revelations have also fueled my passions, especially when I ask the Lord about my children and who they are. He would speak to me about them before they were born, during certain stages in their lives, and even now He still speaks to me about their present and future. The Lord invites me to participate with Him as a father to lead my children to the next phase of the family story, since I am the only one of my siblings married with children. I'm honored that the Lord would use me as a part of the family story to release more generational passion, tenacity, and character that started in my family line well before me.

SCRIPTURAL MEDITATION FOR THE DEPARTMENT OF PASSIONS

For **zeal** for your house has consumed me, and the reproaches of those who reproach you have fallen on me (Psalm 69:9).

Behold my servant, whom I uphold, my chosen, in whom my soul delights; I have put my Spirit upon him; he will bring forth justice to the nations. He will not cry aloud or lift up his voice, or make it heard in the street; a bruised reed he will not break, and a faintly burning wick he will not quench; he will faithfully bring forth justice. **He will not grow faint or be discouraged till he has established justice in the earth**; and the coastlands wait for his law (Isaiah 42:1-4).

So **flee youthful passions** and pursue righteousness, faith, love, and peace, along with those who call on the Lord from a pure heart (2 Timothy 2:22).

For the grace of God has appeared, bringing salvation for all people, training us to **renounce ungodliness and worldly passions**, and to live self-controlled, upright, and godly lives in the present age, waiting for our blessed hope, the appearing of the glory of our great God and Savior Jesus Christ (Titus 2:11-13).

Therefore, since we are surrounded by so great a cloud of witnesses, let us also lay aside every weight, and sin which clings so closely, and **let us run with endurance the race that is set before us**, looking to Jesus, the founder and perfecter of our faith, who for the joy that was set before him endured the cross, despising the shame, and is seated at the right hand of the throne of God (Hebrews 12:1-2).

As obedient children, **do not be conformed to the passions of your former ignorance**, but as he who called you is holy, you also be holy in all your conduct (1 Peter 1:14-15).

CHAPTER ELEVEN LISTENING PRAYER QUESTIONS

1) Lord, what do You need me to know about my Department of Passions?

2) Lord, what am I most passionate about?

3) Lord, what "burns" inside of me?

4) Lord, what am I willing to suffer for?

5) Am I passionate about Your kingdom, or am I more passionate about the systems of the world?

Chapter Twelve

THE DEPARTMENT OF DESIRES
"Allow God to Fulfill Your Desires"

WHAT'S INSIDE THE DEPARTMENT OF DESIRES?

- Delights
- Eagerness
- Expectations
- Cravings
- Hopes
- Longings
- Pleasures
- Pulls
- Yearnings
- Impulses

OVERVIEW OF THE DEPARTMENT

Desires are God-given, and He best orchestrates the fulfillment of these desires.

Let me explain.

I believe that having desires is a part of being human. Desires are natural strong internal longings that motivate us to pursue our needs and wants in life. They are inherently interconnected with our other heart departments, whether we are aware of it or not. Our human desires are related to personal development, relational connections, experiences, lifestyle choices, and a variety of abstract concepts like freedom, power, or influence. These desires aren't bad, yet **how** they are fulfilled can be detrimental to us.

I believe God typically fulfills our desires in relationship with Him and others. In other words, our desires are inherently satisfied relationally. Yet, the challenge is that we may not know our real desires, or we have had negative experiences attached to the fulfillment of real desires, confusing our understanding of what's really happening inside of us. For instance, when I was younger and felt like an outcast in certain communities, those communities were not fulfilling a desire to be accepted. As a result, I resorted to people-pleasing, endurance of verbal abuse and mockery, and other unrighteous behaviors for the sake of getting my desire for acceptance fulfilled. I acted and looked in all the wrong places to fulfill this desire. My experience in trying to fulfill the desire distorted my view of the desire itself, and, at times, I cursed myself and the desire as if something was wrong with me. However, it wasn't that the desire was wrong or bad; it was that the fulfillment of the desire wasn't happening, causing me to seek to fulfill it myself in all the wrong ways.

God created us to have communion with Him and with other humans. In His creative wisdom, He built an environment that fulfilled Adam's desires holistically. They walked together in the garden. Adam was given meaningful work. God gave Adam a woman of His likeness. God collectively gave Adam and Eve reproductive capacity to experience new life, parental authority, and legacy. God established so many things for Adam and Eve to fulfill their desires.

The twist came in humanity when Satan offered humanity an alternative to fulfilling their desires by themselves, which opened the door for pain, destruction, and a change in God's order. Once sin entered the world, our fulfillment of our desires got twisted. Where God was once the ultimate fulfiller of our desires, sin shifted everything and resulted in other speaking spiritual forces (Satan and his demon partners) vying with us to fulfill our desires. Our current fight is about who will we let fulfill our deepest desires.

PRACTICAL STORY

As I have been writing out this book, I have been asking the Lord several questions about my heart. I asked Him one day about my desires, and He walked me through a list of some of my deepest desires. One of those desires He identified was a desire to be accepted. I agreed with Him.

When I was younger, I wanted to be accepted by so many people in my life. Yet, it was hard as a Third Culture Kid[30] growing up in the southern part of the United States. Ethnically, I couldn't fully relate to the cultures of most of my friends. At home, I was different from my siblings. In the community, I had family circumstances that were not the norm. I struggled, and it led me to curse myself and my desire to be accepted. It hurt too much to desire acceptance, so I concluded that I would never be

[30] A Third Culture Kid is a child who was raised in a different culture from their parents for most of their childhood.

accepted and that something was wrong with me. I resorted to careless behaviors that demonstrated how worthless I felt. I struggled with suicidal ideations during high school and late college, and I meditated on frameworks that identified me as someone who would never be understood or accepted by people. Though I have now been a Christian for almost 27 years, the revelation had not hit me until recently that the Lord ultimately wants to fulfill my desire to be accepted. I have lived much of my Christian life with this desire, which resulted in me living in fear of people rejecting me. As the Lord has transformed me, I now regularly repent of seeking to gain people's acceptance, learning instead to embrace the truth that He has fully accepted me in Jesus. God fulfills my deep desires because I choose to delight in Him and His ways.[31]

Out of His goodness and for His glory, He has given me a wife who accepts me as much as a human can accept another human. He has given me children who get to see a picture of a human father, with my own forms of brokenness, who desires to respond to the acceptance and love of His heavenly Father. God has also given me community members who see me, know me, honor me, care for me, and love me to the best of their capacity. I thank the Lord for teaching me how to allow Him to fulfill my desires.

The Lord's heart for us is to delight ourselves in Him, and He will give us the desires of our hearts. This promise from scripture reminds us that our desires are not a problem to be prayed away or removed. Our problem is not with the desires themselves; it is that we don't let God fulfill our deepest desires.

I end this anecdotal section with an example. As you read the example, consider yourself as the child and consider God as the parent:

> A little girl comes to her parents and says, "Mom and Dad, I'm hungry."
>
> Immediately afterwards, the girl, without giving time for response, goes to the refrigerator, opens the door, and looks for the easiest and simplest food to eat. She notices a piece of cheese and starts eating it. Her Mom and Dad look at her with compassion and watch her open the plastic and eat this small piece of cheese they know won't satisfy her hunger.

---

[31] Psalm 37:4

Her mom says to her, “Sweetie, let us make you something to eat.”

The girl retorts, ‘No. I’m good!” as she devours the rest of the cheese and places the last piece in her mouth. She leaves the room and goes back to her previous activities.

This small story exposes a few things:

1. The girl identified her desire.
2. The girl fulfilled her own desire because she felt she was able.
3. The girl rejected her mom’s offer to fulfill the desire.
4. The girl went back to her activities, likely without thinking about what she just did.

Many of our desires are natural like hunger, and we treat God in the same way as the little girl treated her parents. We desire something. We might even pray about it. But we often find a way to quickly fulfill our own desire, dismissing God’s compassionate bid to fulfill the desire, and then we go back to our normal lives. We may live in this cycle for decades and never realize that God wants to faithfully fulfill our desires. We don’t have to repeatedly experience cheapened, unhealthy, destructive, or unsatisfying patterns if we instead choose to let Him take care of us.

SCRIPTURAL MEDITATION FOR THE DEPARTMENT OF DESIRES

O Lord, you **hear the desire of the afflicted**; you will strengthen their heart; you will incline your ear to do justice to the fatherless and the oppressed, so that man who is of the earth may strike terror no more (Psalm 10:17-18).

May we shout for joy over your salvation, and in the name of our God set up our banners! **May the Lord fulfill all your petitions**! (Psalm 20:5).

You have given him his **heart's desire** and have not withheld the **request of his lips**. *Selah.* For you meet him with rich blessings; you set a crown of fine gold upon his head. He asked life of you; you gave it to him, length of days forever and ever (Psalm 21:2-4).

Delight yourself in the Lord, and he will give you **the desires of your heart** (Psalm 37:4).

Hope deferred makes the heart sick, but a **desire fulfilled** is a tree of life (Proverbs 13:12).

CHAPTER TWELVE LISTENING PRAYER

1) Lord, what do You need me to know about this Department of Desires?

2) Lord, what are some of my deepest desires?

3) Lord, will You give me some examples of how You want to fulfill my desires?

4) Lord, how am I fulfilling desires for myself and not allowing You to fulfill them?

5) Lord, what are some scriptural meditations I need to help train me in letting You fulfill my desires?

Chapter Thirteen

THE DEPARTMENT OF CONSCIENCE
"Don't Dishonor Your Conscience"

WHAT'S INSIDE THE DEPARTMENT OF CONSCIENCE?

- Beliefs
- Convictions
- Judgments
- Laws
- Rules
- Standards
- Values

DEPARTMENT OVERVIEW

The laws, statutes, commandments, and ways of the Lord are written on the new hearts given to those who have received the gospel of Jesus Christ. The Lord writes His law on every new heart He gives to those who believe, in accordance with His promise to them. Here is how the prophet Jeremiah shares God's intentions:

> Behold, the days are coming, declares the Lord, when I will make a new covenant with the house of Israel and the house of Judah, not like the covenant that I made with their fathers on the day when I took them by the hand to bring them out of the land of Egypt, my covenant that they broke, though I was their husband, declares the Lord. For this is the covenant that I will make with the house of Israel after those days, declares the Lord: I will put my law within them, and I will write it on their hearts. And I will be their God, and they shall be my people. And no longer shall each one teach his neighbor and each his brother, saying, 'Know the Lord,' for they shall all know me, from the least of them to the greatest, declares the Lord. For I will forgive their iniquity, and I will remember their sin no more (Jeremiah 31:31-34).

The core of God's message is that humans cannot fulfill the purposes of God with their own human convictions or standards; the Lord had to embed His laws in the human heart.

Our convictions, beliefs, rules, judgments, and standards of living all operate in this Department of Conscience. The new heart God gave to us who believe in Jesus has everything needed for a life of godliness. Most of our journey as believers is to allow God's words to renew our previous perspectives on how we see life, welcoming the fullest of this new heart to have its way with us. The new upgraded heart is quite powerful. Consider what the Apostle Peter says in his letter:

> His divine power has granted to us all things that pertain to life and godliness, through the knowledge of him who called us to his own glory and excellence, by which he has granted to us his precious and very great promises, so that through them you may become partakers of the divine nature, having escaped from the corruption that is in the world because of sinful desire.
> (2 Peter 1:3-4)

Through the new heart, we get a new conscience, which we do not want to sear[32] or dishonor because it is a gift to allow us to live according to God's way.

PRACTICAL STORY

Before I became a believer, the things I regularly did seemed normal to me. But after I became a new believer and offered my life to the Lord, I began to feel convicted about those old habits. It was a strange feeling, at first I thought something was wrong with me. The reality was that I had a new heart, and Holy Spirit was present in my life. The closer I grew to the Lord, the less I could continue to do some of the things I had done in the past because my conscience had been turned on at a level that I had not experienced before.

Here is a specific example: Before I met the Lord, I had quite a foul mouth. I grew up in a context that welcomed all kinds of vulgarities and obscenities as a normal part of everyday speech. I, likewise, adopted the patterns of my environment. After I became a believer at 18 years old, I felt guilty for the first time about using language that dishonored the Lord, but I felt I couldn't stop speaking that way. However, within the first few years after my experience with Jesus, my values changed with longing to want to honor Him with my speech. My speech patterns began to change, for I welcomed God's word to fill, convict, permeate, and change my life from the inside out. I was amazed at the transformation.

---

[32] 1 Timothy 4:2

What I have learned over the years is that the nearer I am to the Lord, the more sensitive I am to His ways, commandments, instructions, and patterns. I tend to want to please Him more through believing what He says about me, and I allow Him to have His way with me more often. I feel more of His conviction about who I am and things I'm doing wrong and find myself challenged to do things His way. This Department of Conscience keeps me within the boundaries and parameters of God's will and purposes for my life.

SCRIPTURAL MEDITATION FOR THE DEPARTMENT OF CONSCIENCE

...Then David arose and stealthily cut off a corner of Saul's robe. And afterward **David's heart struck him**, because he had cut off a corner of Saul's robe. He said to his men, "The Lord forbid that I should do this thing to my lord, the Lord's anointed, to put out my hand against him, seeing he is the Lord's anointed (1 Samuel 24:4-6).

But **David's heart struck him** after he had numbered the people. And David said to the Lord, "I have sinned greatly in what I have done. But now, O Lord, please take away the iniquity of your servant, for I have done very foolishly (2 Samuel 24:10).

Nevertheless, I tell you the truth: it is to your advantage that I go away, for if I do not go away, the Helper will not come to you. But if I go, I will send him to you. And when he comes, **he will convict** the world concerning sin and righteousness and judgment... (John 16:7-8).

Let all the house of Israel therefore know for certain that God has made him both Lord and Christ, this Jesus whom you crucified. Now when they heard this **they were cut to the heart**, and said to Peter and the rest of the apostles, "Brothers, what shall we do?" And Peter said to them, "Repent and be baptized every one of you in the name of Jesus Christ for the forgiveness of your sins, and you will receive the gift of the Holy Spirit (Acts 2:36-38).

CHAPTER THIRTEEN LISTENING PRAYER

1) Lord, what do You need me to know about this department of my conscience?

2) Lord, will You reveal any things that are on my conscience that I need to confess?

3) Lord, whose standards am I living by, Yours or the world's?

4) Lord, what do I believe? What are my values?

5) Lord, what more do You want to say to me regarding my conscience?

Chapter Fourteen

THE DEPARTMENT OF CHARACTER
"Walk in the Fullness of Character"

WHAT'S INSIDE THE DEPARTMENT OF CHARACTER?

- Behavior
- Identity
- Lifestyle
- Role-playing
- Fruit of the Spirit[33]

DEPARTMENT OVERVIEW

There are several times in the scriptures where people were identified by the character of their hearts, being described as blameless, righteous, or wicked. It seems to imply that there are character traits associated with the heart based on the lifestyle choices of the person. For instance, when God created Adam and Eve, they were each fully aligned in their character before sin entered the world. God treated them accordingly. They were responsive to God accordingly, and they lived in God's peace accordingly. Yet, when sin entered both of them, something shifted. They covered themselves. They hid from God. They blamed others and did not take responsibility for their actions. **Their whole world changed.**

Even in their next generation of children, God spoke to Cain about what was happening in his heart toward his brother. God identified that something separate from him, called "sin", was the root thing he would have to master. Sin was crouching at his door ready to pounce on him, and Cain seemingly had the capacity to master the sin coming after him.[34] It was as if God saw his capacity, ability, and design, yet sin was waiting for the opportunity to affect Cain's life. It seems that Cain opened the door through his anger, which led to the murder of his brother Abel. I believe, based on God's statements to Cain, that God knows how to separate our true selves from our sin.

---

[33] Galatians 5:22

[34] Genesis 4:3-7

In the Bible, a number of people were classified as having good character but were not perfect people. Job was considered a man who was blameless and upright, for he feared God and shunned evil.[35] God blessed Job, for Job did not curse God when he was under pressure. However, Job did not have the most perfect perspective of God.[36] Noah was considered a righteous man and blameless, walking faithfully with God.[37] Yet, after Noah came out of the ark, he became drunk.[38] Although King David sought after the heart of God, he murdered one of his military men after sleeping with that soldier's wife.[39] God used all of these men faithfully to fulfill His purposes, yet each man was imperfect. However, their manifestations of sin did not determine their holistic character.

God saw something in their hearts in spite of their mistakes and human shortcomings. I believe that we can walk in the identity of God, but still have to work out our character. I also believe God views us according to our true identity, not according to our sin. God deals with our sin according to His justice and purpose, but does not condemn the person who is in relationship with Jesus.

This heart department is best understood through intimacy with God and through His revelations of who we are over the course of life. Consider two men, Jeremiah and Paul, who each had their identity, role, and purpose in life revealed to them:

Example 1: The Prophet Jeremiah

> The word of the Lord came to me, saying, "Before I formed you in the womb I knew you, before you were born I set you apart; I appointed you as a prophet to the nations."
>
> "Alas, Sovereign Lord," I said, "I do not know how to speak; I am too young."
>
> But the Lord said to me, "Do not say, 'I am too young.' You must go to everyone I send you to and say whatever I command you.

[35] Job 1:8

[36] Job 42:1-6

[37] Gen. 6:9

[38] Gen. 9:20-21

[39] 2 Samuel 12:9-1

> Do not be afraid of them, for I am with you and will rescue you," declares the Lord" (Jeremiah 1:4-8, NIV).

Notice that God speaks to Jeremiah and gives him his identity of why he was created, yet Jeremiah pushed back and looked at his condition and status as a child. I am not sure Jeremiah realized that God's identity and calling were not determined by his status and conditions. God, as the storyteller, knew Jeremiah before he even existed.

Similarly, let's look at the Apostle Paul's articulation of who he is. Paul wrote this information to his spiritual son, Timothy.

<u>Example 2</u>: The Apostle Paul

> For there is one God and one mediator between God and mankind, the man Christ Jesus, who gave himself as a ransom for all people. This has now been witnessed to at the proper time. And for this purpose I was appointed a herald and an apostle—I am telling the truth, I am not lying—and a true and faithful teacher of the Gentiles (1 Timothy 2:5-7, NIV).
>
> He has saved us and called us to a holy life—not because of anything we have done but because of his own purpose and grace. This grace was given us in Christ Jesus before the beginning of time, but it has now been revealed through the appearing of our Savior, Christ Jesus, who has destroyed death and has brought life and immortality to light through the gospel. And of this gospel I was appointed a herald and an apostle and a teacher. That is why I am suffering as I am. Yet this is no cause for shame, because I know whom I have believed, and am convinced that he is able to guard what I have entrusted to him until that day (2 Timothy 1:9-12, NIV).

I ask you to consider how clearly Paul was able to articulate his identity to his son in the faith, Timothy. Paul identified himself as one appointed to be a herald, apostle, and teacher by the gospel. Paul seemed so sure of his identity. I believe that since Paul knew his identity, he also understood his suffering.

PRACTICAL STORY

I relate to these biblical figures in my own life, for I know the moments where I felt unqualified because of my sin, but God still used me for His purposes. A scripture that gives me comfort is a part of King David's prayer in Psalm 23:3 "...he leads me in paths of righteousness for his name's sake." I recognize that many of the things I have going right for me are based on God's choice to establish me as righteous, and He does things in me for **His name's sake**. In essence, anytime we are being led in paths of righteousness, it is about His name, His purposes, His story, His glory, and His Kingdom agenda. I am honored to participate in His divine nature, yet I cannot take credit for "doing" anything to change myself. I embrace the fact that my life is designed to glorify God, not myself.

Some of the most powerful moments in my life came during times when I was at my weakest: discouraged, feeling alone, feeling rejected, or extremely vulnerable. As I continued to live in those humbled states, I became more comfortably uncomfortable. In other words, I learned to embody feeling uneasy about trusting God in hard circumstances or when I did not know the outcome of a matter. My faith muscles got their best workouts when I was not in my best human strength. Many of my stories are connected to what the Apostle Paul said to the Corinthian church,

> For consider your calling, brothers: not many of you were wise according to worldly standards, not many were powerful, not many were of noble birth. But God chose what is foolish in the world to shame the wise; God chose what is weak in the world to shame the strong; God chose what is low and despised in the world, even things that are not, to bring to nothing things that are, so that no human being might boast in the presence of God. And because of him you are in Christ Jesus, who became to us wisdom from God, righteousness and sanctification and redemption, so that, as it is written, "Let the one who boasts, boast in the Lord" (1 Corinthians 1:26-31).

I reflect and it makes me thankful that I am not able to take credit for the powerful manifestations of the power of God in my life. I know I am weak in my humanity, but righteous and holy in God's sight. My identity has been established by the grace of God, and I grow in the character of Christ. If fact, I relate to the Apostle Paul's statements over his life all the time:

> For I am the least of the apostles, unworthy to be called an apostle, because I persecuted the church of God. But by the grace of God I am what I am, and his grace toward me was not in vain.

> On the contrary, I worked harder than any of them, though it was not I, but the grace of God that is with me (1 Corinthians 15:9-10).

When we embrace that our identity is rooted in the grace of God, something inside of us changes. We begin to embrace the purposes of God and live in the character of Jesus.

SCRIPTURAL MEDITATION FOR THE DEPARTMENT OF CHARACTER

Not because of your **righteousness or the uprightness of your heart** are you going in to possess their land, but because of the wickedness of these nations the Lord your God is driving them out from before you, and that he may confirm the word that the Lord swore to your fathers, to Abraham, to Isaac, and to Jacob" (Deuteronomy 9:5).

And Solomon said, "You have shown great and steadfast love to your servant David my father, because he walked before you in faithfulness, in righteousness, and **in uprightness of heart** toward you. And you have kept for him this great and steadfast love and have given him a son to sit on his throne this day. And now, O Lord my God, you have made your servant king in place of David my father, although I am but a little child. I do not know how to go out or come in. And your servant is in the midst of your people whom you have chosen, a great people, too many to be numbered or counted for multitude. Give your servant therefore an understanding mind to govern your people, that I may discern between good and evil, for who is able to govern this your great people? (1 Kings 3:6-9).

My words declare the **uprightness of my heart**, and what my lips know they speak sincerely (Job 33:3).

What then did you go out to see? A prophet? Yes, I tell you, and more than a prophet. This is he of whom it is written,

> 'Behold, I send my messenger before your face, who will prepare your way before you.'

Truly, I say to you, among those born of women there has arisen **no one greater than John the Baptist**. Yet the one who is **least in the kingdom** of heaven is greater than he" (Matthew 11:9-11).

And Jesus answered him, "Blessed are you, Simon Bar-Jonah! For flesh and blood has not revealed this to you, but my Father who is in heaven.

And I tell you, **you are Peter**[40], and on this rock I will build my church, and the gates of hell shall not prevail against it. I will give you the keys of the kingdom of heaven, and whatever you bind on earth shall be bound in heaven, and whatever you loose on earth shall be loosed in heaven (Matthew 16:17-19).

CHAPTER FOURTEEN LISTENING PRAYER

1) Lord, who am I?

2) Lord, what do You call me?

3) Lord, which ministry roles identified in Ephesians 4:11-13 best fit my identity? Will You explain?

4) Lord, will You reveal my character to me so I can see what You see?

5) Lord, what do You want to further say about me?

6) Lord, what fruit of the Spirit in Galatians 5:22-23 are You working to develop in me?

---

[40] Throughout scripture, we often see the Lord giving someone a new name, representing a new identity He has given them. See other examples in Gen. 17:5, Gen. 32:28, and 2 Samuel 12:24-25.

Chapter Fifteen

THE DEPARTMENT OF WILL

"Decide Toward the Things of God."

WHAT'S INSIDE THE DEPARTMENT OF WILL?

- Decision-Making
- Guidance
- Direction
- Wishes
- Agenda
- Pleasure
- Plans
- Desire

DEPARTMENT OVERVIEW

Seeking, knowing, and living in the will of God is the most important aspiration for every human being.

Consider a manufacturer of a consumer good:

A manufacturer chooses to take raw materials and transform them into a new product to sell on the market. The manufacturer envisions that the end product will transform an entire community by enhancing people's lives for decades. The price is paid for the raw materials. The transformation and production happen over time. The quality control team tests the final product, and the consumer good is now on the market. The benefits begin after the exchange of money for the sold item.

If we were to consider ourselves as if we were a consumer good, we could see the heart of God as the manufacturer. God chooses us in our raw and broken state. He decides to transform us into purposeful children of God. He tests our faith and sets us in places that bring life and benefit to others. Our lives become a blessing to those who receive what the Lord has done with us.

This is the will of God: To fulfill His agenda for our lives on the earth.

Yet, there is one major caveat.

Unlike inanimate objects, we as humans were given a will from God that enables us to decide and choose for ourselves. This power of choice can be trained toward righteousness or unrighteousness. We can choose to listen to truth or falsehood. We can choose to obey or disobey. Our power of choice can reinforce or hinder God's agenda for our lives.

Consider the Apostle Paul's words in Romans 12:2:

> "Do not be conformed to this world, but be transformed by the renewal of your mind, that by testing you may discern what is the will of God, what is good and acceptable and perfect."

From what I gather from this scripture, it seems like we must choose to renew our minds and allow for testing so that we can distinguish what God's will is for our lives. If we have been self-centered for most of our lives, we must renew our minds according to God's ways in order to discern His will. Also, if we have been trained to meditate on unrighteous things, we will need to learn to meditate on righteous things to learn of God's will. Paul's words communicate volumes to all of us, especially if we desire to know God's good, pleasing, and acceptable will.

PRACTICAL STORY

Growing up, I did not get to make many major decisions for my life. My father led each of his children toward getting good marks in school, playing competitive sports, and going off to college. We were all award-winning athletes in high school and college and completed multiple college degrees, with eight total degrees among the three of us. Our life direction was scripted academically and athletically, yet our emotions, passions, and other relational aspects of our lives were not so directed.

My sister, my brother, and I each pursued chemistry as our field of study for our undergraduate program, influenced by our chemist father. Yet, during my studies, I made a choice not to pursue chemistry as a profession. I was choosing to break the mold, which represented a major decision.

I recognized at the beginning of my second year that chemistry was not for me. I sensed my desires unfulfilled by the prospect of becoming a chemist. My emotions communicated loudly every time I was in my organic chemistry lab class; I started to hate chemistry and wanted to break every test tube and beaker out of frustration. My salvation, which I had experienced the prior semester, awakened my passions for the things of God, and I realized that my character would be hollow if I continued pursuing something I no longer liked. I was in a place of crisis because my heart had changed from pursuing my earthly father's dream to my Heavenly Father's dream.

I need to note that during this period of my life, I constantly wrestled with my will and had several questions emerge:

Do I keep pursuing what I was told to do?

What will happen if I change directions?

What will my parents think? What will other people think of me?

If I don't do chemistry, what will I do with my life?

How will I make money?

Can I really trust God in this journey?

What is God's will for my life?

In time, I chose God's path to seek out what He had for me. I decided to finish my chemistry degree for logistical reasons, as I was on a chemistry scholarship. I chose to pursue a second major in religious studies with an emphasis on Christian studies, and I decided not to pursue a career in chemistry. I chose to seek temporary employment at an agency to earn some money as I wrestled through that period, and I finally landed a job as an office associate in a newly created academic department at my university. This job provided stability in my life, trained my general and administrative skills, and offered opportunities that undergird almost everything I do now in my 20+ year professional career.

God graciously transformed the direction of my life in those three years. Here are some of the benefits I received at that time:

- The university paid for my Master of Arts in Communication Studies.
- I hired and supervised student employees.
- I managed much of the departmental budget.
- I assisted in the administration of the office affairs.
- I helped develop an innovative master's program.

- I worked with several seasoned faculty and staff members on several projects.
- I taught my first semester-long university course and much more.

God knew the direction He had for me. I am so grateful that I left the world of chemistry and started in a new direction. In fact, most of my career has been the Lord preparing me for leadership, training others, and empowering others. He has given me wisdom and understanding of who I am in Him, and because of this, I can now recognize and embrace the risk of not always knowing the direction of my life. I regularly renew my mind, and I keep practicing how to make decisions focused on doing God's will for my life rather than my own will.

SCRIPTURAL MEDITATION FOR THE DEPARTMENT OF WILL

And he humbled you and let you hunger and fed you with manna, which you did not know, nor did your fathers know, that he might make you know that man does not live by bread alone, but **man lives by every word that comes from the mouth of the Lord** (Deuteronomy 8:3).

Your word is a lamp to my feet and a light to my path. I have sworn an oath and confirmed it, to keep your righteous rules (Psalm 119:105-106).

Then Jesus was led up by the Spirit into the wilderness to be tempted by the devil. And after fasting forty days and forty nights, he was hungry. And the tempter came and said to him, "If you are the Son of God, command these stones to become loaves of bread." But he answered, "It is written, '**Man shall not live by bread alone, but by every word that comes from the mouth of God**'" (Matthew 4:1-4).

Then Jesus went with them to a place called Gethsemane, and he said to his disciples, "Sit here, while I go over there and pray." And taking with him Peter and the two sons of Zebedee, he began to be sorrowful and troubled. Then he said to them, "My soul is very sorrowful, even to death; remain here, and watch with me." And going a little farther he fell on his face and prayed, saying, "My Father, if it be possible, let this cup pass from me; nevertheless, **not as I will, but as you will**." And he came to the disciples and found them sleeping. And he said to Peter, "So, could you not watch with me one hour? Watch and pray that you may not enter into temptation. The spirit indeed is willing, but the flesh is weak." Again, for the second time, he went away and prayed, "My Father, if this cannot pass unless I drink it, **your will be done**." And again he came and found them sleeping, for their eyes were heavy. So, leaving them again, he went away and prayed for the third time, saying the same words again (Matthew 26:36-44).

I appeal to you therefore, brothers, by the mercies of God, to present your bodies as a living sacrifice, holy and acceptable to God, which is your spiritual worship. Do not be conformed to this world, but be transformed by the renewal of your mind, that by testing **you may discern what is the will of God, what is good and acceptable and perfect** (Romans 12:1-2).

CHAPTER FIFTEEN LISTENING PRAYER

1) Lord, what is Your will for my life?

2) Lord, where are the areas of my life that I have yet to submit to Your will?

3) Lord, who really leads my life? Let Your Word lead my life.

4) Lord, will You help me to pray the Lord's prayer of Matthew 6:9-13 with a sincere heart?

5) Is there anything else You want to share with me about **my** will?

6) Is there anything else You want to share with me about **Your** will?

Chapter Sixteen

PRACTICALLY INTEGRATING ALL OF THE DEPARTMENTS

We are now at the place of final descent, not unlike an airplane landing on the runway. I use this word-picture of an airplane because much of this last portion of the book has been communicated conceptually, abstractly, and at a 30,000-foot level. We've been somewhat "high in the sky", traveling from one place of insight to another on how the heart functions.

I now need us to be ready to consider how to live all of this out in a practical, integrative, and purposeful way.

Let me start with the reminder of what I sensed the Lord shared with me:

> **"Train your mind.**
> **Lead your emotions and feelings.**
> **Fully give yourself to your passions.**
> **Allow Me to fulfill your desires.**
> **Don't dishonor your conscience.**
> **Walk in the fullness of character.**
> **Decide toward the things of God. May My will be done."**

We have learned several different concepts related to the human heart. I've shared anecdotes about my personal life related to my own journey of understanding. I've given fundamentals of the heart and outlined my conception of the different heart departments of this central headquarters of life. I now want to end with sharing some practical thoughts in how to train and navigate our hearts and with offering some encouragement to remain faithful to the framework that I sensed the Lord shared with me.

For all of your life, you have been regularly training your mind. You've been inundated with knowledge, information, and things that have repeated over and over again for memorization, such as the pledges, songs, slogans, jingles, and much more.

When I speak about the need to train your mind, I'm not referring to training your thinking capacity to know more information, but rather, evaluating and potentially changing the goal of your training. The challenge is that your Department of Intellect likely hasn't been trained toward the things of God or in the ways of God, but primarily toward the things of your culture. You may have volumes of training in Christian activities, such as Bible verse memorization, listening to once-a-week Sunday sermons, or patterns based on liturgical traditions, but have these actions actually changed your lifestyle to live in God's power?

I am referring to a training that teaches you to think as God thinks and to show you how to walk in God's ways, which is an intimate relational training. I am talking about how you let go of your cultural patterns of thinking and offer your whole self to the Lord, by letting Him teach, lead, guide, and show you who you are in Him. I am also referring to how you put in the intentional time to train your meditations, just as you might do with your media consumption, your educational pursuits, your job expectations, and your other devotions in life.

Are you willing to commit yourself to seeking God to learn from Him about His ways?

Are you willing to allow God to train you on how He wants you to intellectually process the details of your life?

It's time to intentionally train our minds by the thoughts of God and the ways of God through the study of His Word, intimate prayer time with Him, scriptural meditations, listening to Spirit-filled, trustworthy leaders and preachers, and, as I have already suggested in this book, listening prayer questions. These action steps will help you grow in your ability to love the Lord with your mind,[41] deepen your intimacy with God, and love people better. This department is trained best in community with others who can help you discern what the Lord is communicating to you.

---

[41] Mark 12:30; Luke 10:27

THE ULTIMATE GOAL OF TRAINING YOUR MIND

Friend, this department is so important, for it is a starting place to see your heart change. The goal is that as you seek the Lord's ways of thinking, this department will develop and begin to help you learn how to lead your emotions better, give life to your passions, allow God to fulfill your desires, honor your conscience, walk in full character, and know His will for your life.

PRACTICAL LISTENING PRAYER QUESTIONS FOR THE DEPARTMENT OF INTELLECT

1) Lord, what are some practical ways I can train my intellect?

2) Lord, what are some distractions that keep me from focusing on You?

3) Lord, what are some strategies to help me read my Bible more?

4) Lord, what are some strategies to help me spend more time with You?

Remember, your emotions are like indicator lights on the dashboard of a car.

They will illuminate.
You will "feel the feels."
It's okay to emote.

However, be careful not to ignore your emotions, but rather to lead them to the truth of what Jesus would say about your emotions or feelings, such as fear, rejection, shame, hurt, hopelessness, disappointment, or whatever other emotion or feeling you are having. The exercise of leading your emotions will take work and likely cost you something.

I don't believe many cultures train emotions well, especially western cultures. In fact, I believe we are becoming increasingly masterful at numbing our emotions by allowing false comforters of media consumption, entertainment, addictions, and avoidance to make us feel momentarily better but not actually become better. Because of this poor training, I encourage you to "feel the feels" and learn how to walk through your feelings and emotions rather than numb them. I recommend creating times in your day to invite God to bring you comfort. I recommend courageously finding trusted brothers and sisters in the Lord who can allow you to vent for moments so that you can practice sharing, expressing, and releasing your emotions. It might cost you some discomfort, a few moments of feeling embarrassed, and perhaps even shedding some tears, but it will pay dividends as you begin living a life of emotional health and wholeness.

THE ULTIMATE GOAL OF LEADING YOUR EMOTIONS AND FEELINGS

A healthy emotional department heightens your spiritual sensitivity to God and to the people around you. Since you have a human spirit, and your connection to God is through Holy Spirit, who also has emotions and feelings, you may begin to feel things the same way God feels as you become healthier. Further, you will likely increase in your discernment, in sensing God's presence, and in feeling things at supernatural levels. The breath from Holy Spirit inside of you will spark your emotions and feelings to illuminate, and the goal will be to allow God, your Comforter, to help you navigate what's happening inside of you. **Please do not dismiss your emotions and feelings, or you may miss God's communication!** The Lord may speak to you directly or use your community to help you lead these important emotional communicators. Again, the healthier you become, the more integrated into the spirit realm you'll be because of the balance between your physical earthly experiences with your spiritual experiences.

PRACTICAL LISTENING PRAYER QUESTIONS FOR THE DEPARTMENT OF EMOTIONS AND FEELINGS

1) Lord, will You show me specific scriptures that will help me with my emotions and feelings?

2) Lord, will You reveal the ways You want to comfort me when I'm feeling big emotions?

3) Lord, what are my false comforters currently in my life? How do You want me to deal with them?

4) What do You want me to know about these false comforters? What have they been doing to my life?

5) Lord, will You show me how to make You my chief Comforter?

FULLY GIVING YOURSELF TO YOUR PASSIONS

As I write this, I sense that this department can be a scary place for some people. You may have been told your whole life that you are too strong or too passionate in your personality, or that you're too much to handle. The truth is that you likely have a deep passion within that God has given you to express to the world. I would recommend that you give yourself to it, but first, do your due diligence to understand your passions and why He gave them to you. Ask God to simply confirm and articulate what's happening inside of you. You want to be very clear about how you sacrifice and give yourself over to the things of God.

Whatever He says about your passions is an indication of His calling for your life, and He will teach you how to wrestle with your calling. Your calling is the invitation from God to fulfill purposes that are far beyond your ability, yet He'll be with you through your journey. I suggest you take this process step by step and learn to let Him lead you.

THE ULTIMATE GOAL OF FULLY GIVING YOURSELF TO YOUR PASSIONS

Your unique passions are the gift that you give to the world. If you attempt to walk in someone else's calling, you'll miss what's unique to you. Thus, the ultimate aim here is to be responsive to the specific invitation that God has given to you so that you walk in the gift you are to those that God has entrusted to you.

PRACTICAL LISTENING PRAYER QUESTIONS FOR THE DEPARTMENT OF PASSIONS

1) Lord, what are my deep passions? How are they displayed to the world right now?

2) Lord, what are You inviting me into at this stage of my life?

3) Lord, how do You want me to respond to this invitation?

4) Lord, what do You want me to give up?

5) Lord, who are the people entrusted to me?

6) Lord, will You show me ways to live fully into my passions?

Recently, I did an informal study with some friends, and I asked them to ask the Lord about their desires. Overwhelmingly, each person used the word "trust" in their responses (of note: they did not talk to each other; it was from the Lord). Here are some of the verbatim responses as they prayed and asked the Lord about their specific desires:

> "Trust the process."
> "Trust Me."
> "Trust."
> "You have to trust Me..."
> "Continue to trust Me with these desires."
> "Trust my timeline, my protection, my leading..."

I sense the Lord is seriously inviting us to trust Him, which suggests He does not view our desires negatively. Based on my own experience and on some of my friends' processing with the Lord, I continue to conclude that it is a good thing to have desires. Yet, it is important not to let our own fulfillment of that desire be a stumbling block. It appears that God wants to show us how to trust Him to fulfill our desires.

I encourage you not to curse your desires or ask God to take them away. Be careful about saying or praying things like,

> "Why am I like this?"
>
> "I hate this part of myself."
>
> "I'm so stupid to want this thing again. God must not want this desire for me."
>
> "What is wrong with me to want this so much?"
>
> "Lord, take this desire away from me. I don't want it."

I believe your core underlying desires are good, but because we may have tried to fulfill them on our own, or they have become twisted by sinful activity, they may have brought pain or frustration. Thus, we say or pray the above out of hurt or hopelessness. Remember, it's not that the core desire is bad and needs to go away; it's that we must learn to continue to trust God to fulfill our desires. What I just said is easy, but it requires faith to trust God on the journey to fulfillment.

You likely have a desire to be loved, appreciated, respected, and cared for in your life. I encourage you not to look to fulfill these desires in all the wrong places, such as multiple dating relationships, inappropriate sexual activities, endless scrolling on social media, or workaholism. In the end, those activities won't fulfill your desires.

God already has a chosen community for you.[42]
God will give you life-giving, intimate relationships.
God knows the depth of your desires.[43]
God already loves, appreciates, respects, and cares for you.
God does not want you to strive for these things; He wants to reveal how He meets these desires.[44]

Will you allow Him to reveal to you how He wants to fulfill your desires?

THE ULTIMATE GOAL OF ALLOWING GOD TO FULFILL YOUR DESIRES

The goal is to train yourself to allow God, who placed the desires within you, to demonstrate His faithfulness to you. He wants to give you the desires of your heart. So, I encourage you to review, meditate on, and rehearse the scripture in Psalms 37:4 as a guide when you consider your desires. The scripture says, "Delight yourself in the Lord, and he will give you the desires of your heart."

Will you make it your aim to delight in the Lord and trust His faithfulness to fulfill your desires?

PRACTICAL LISTENING PRAYER QUESTIONS FOR THE DEPARTMENT OF DESIRES

1) Lord, will You show me one specific desire You want me to notice?

---

[42] Psalm 68:5-6 (NIV): "A father to the fatherless, a defender of widows, is God in his holy dwelling. God sets the lonely in families, he leads out the prisoners with singing..."

[43] Psalm 139:1; 139:23: " O Lord, you have searched me and known me!" "... Search me, O God, and know my heart! Try me and know my thoughts! And see if there be any grievous way in me, and lead me in the way everlasting!"

[44] Psalm 23:1-3: "The Lord is my shepherd; I shall not want. He makes me lie down in green pastures. He leads me beside still waters. He restores my soul..."

2) Lord, how have I attempted to fulfill this desire?

3) Lord, how have I cursed or devalued this desire?

4) Lord, how do You want to fulfill this desire?

5) Lord, how do You view this desire? What do You want to say about it?

You and I have deep convictions, values, and beliefs that lead our lives. If you were to ask the Lord about those values, convictions, and beliefs, He'd have a lot to say. To be clear, I am not talking about what you cognitively know from the Bible and all the things that sound right and good as a Christian. I am talking about what you really believe by way of your actions and duties. If you genuinely believe something, you will live a lifestyle that reflects that.

Your conscience is such an important part of your heart, so please do not ignore, belittle, minimize, or lower the value of the warning signs your conscience gives you. I recommend engaging God about your values, beliefs, and convictions, especially when you get gut feelings, "checks in your spirit," a variety of hunches, or "bad vibes" about a person or a circumstance. Talk with God as your Father to gain clarity about what's happening inside of you in those moments, honoring your conscience. This department is your anchor in staying on the straight and narrow path you will walk on.

THE ULTIMATE GOAL OF HONORING YOUR CONSCIENCE

As you practically consider how to honor your conscience, one of the most important things to note is that you do not want to sear your conscience. A seared conscience is likened to the burning of your skin or a callus on one of your toes, for once the nerve endings of the skin get damaged, you would have no warning of danger or problems. Someone with this kind of damage could place their hand on a hot stove, and they would burn themselves, for they would not know how to jerk their hand away.

Consider the application of the above in context of the Apostle Paul's words to Timothy:

> Now the Spirit expressly says that in later times some will depart from the faith by devoting themselves to deceitful spirits and teachings of demons, through the insincerity of liars whose consciences are seared, who forbid marriage and require abstinence from foods that God created to be received with thanksgiving by those who believe and know the truth (1 Timothy 4:1-3).

I believe Paul's words inform us of the danger of having a seared conscience in life. If you consistently ignore Holy Spirit's warning signs or perpetually respond to Him with numbness, your conscience will grow increasingly unfeeling and insensitive and eventually become seared. A seared conscience can lead you to lying or even devoting yourself to deceitful spirits and the teachings of demons. It can also lead you to reject things like marriage that God considers good.

God has given us the beautiful gift of the conscience to keep us focused and moving toward the things of God rather than away from the things of God. Ultimately, the goal is to keep your conscience tender and sensitive to the Spirit of the Lord.

PRACTICAL LISTENING PRAYER QUESTIONS FOR THE DEPARTMENT OF CONSCIENCE

(Positive warning: These questions may trigger deep levels of conviction.)

1) Lord, what is an example of one of my beliefs?

2) Lord, will You show me how my lifestyle actions match this belief?

3) Lord, where are the areas of my life where my conscience is seared or in danger of becoming seared?

4) Lord, will You heal my conscience and restore my sensitivity to Holy Spirit and the things You have for me?

5) Is there anything else You want me to know about my beliefs or my conscience?

Imagine yourself as an actor in a play, and you've been chosen as the main character. You have many things to practice. You spend the necessary time training yourself by memorizing your lines, practicing your stage presence, your timing, and all the things required of you. As you rehearse, you visualize yourself on stage and embody your character. In time, you become the character.

Similarly, God has chosen you to be a part of His play, for He desires for you to have a specific role in life.

Will you function as the main character in the story God has for you?

Will you learn your role in life?

Will you remember and meditate on what He says about you?

Will you walk in the fullness of the character that He has for you?

When we all fully embrace our identities and walk in the fullness of the character we are called to, everything works smoothly. God's story is displayed to the world in such a way that other people may want to watch and participate in God's masterpiece. They will observe you and me as Jesus followers who are committed to being coached and trained by God to be the best that we can be, even in the midst of our own brokenness and problems. God uses us as ambassadors, and He reinforces our testimonies of how He has trained us to be who we are. We get to participate in God's bigger story by giving Him the glory and praise for our lives.

Will you join God in His mission and be the best that you can be?

THE ULTIMATE GOAL OF WALKING IN THE FULLNESS OF YOUR CHARACTER

Often, we look at character in terms of good or bad; in essence, the focus is on judging character. When we focus on judging a person's character, we can infer that the development and growth of a person at a single point in their life are complete. However, we were not meant to be the standard-bearers of what is good or bad character, and in our attempts to act as such, we can dismiss a person who has not fully developed the character God expects. We must all remember that God is the Author and Finisher of one's faith.[45] He alone is the One who completes the work that He started in people.[46] He is the ultimate judge.[47]

We would be better served by focusing on training our character in the role God has given to us uniquely and individually. When you focus here, many people will be watching you. Their hearts will be affected because God will display the beauty of who you are uniquely to the world. You become a gift to others, thereby giving people the opportunity to witness a life well-coached, directed, and led by the Lord. It's inspiring to watch people walking in their true identity.

The goal of walking in the fullness of your character is to learn of your identity and fulfill your role in life that God has for you. If you do so, you will receive the great rewards of God.

PRACTICAL LISTENING PRAYER QUESTIONS FOR THE DEPARTMENT OF CHARACTER

1) Lord, based on what You call me, how do I walk in my God-given identity?

2) Lord, what is my role in ______ situation? (For ________, consider one of your contexts in life: family, school, work, community.)

3) Lord, what are my spiritual gifts? (You can consider taking spiritual gift assessments.)

---

[45] Hebrews 12:1-2: "Therefore, since we are surrounded by so great a cloud of witnesses, let us also lay aside every weight, and sin which clings so closely, and let us run with endurance the race that is set before us, looking to Jesus, the founder and perfecter of our faith...

[46] Philippians 1:6: "And I am sure of this, that he who began a good work in you will bring it to completion at the day of Jesus Christ."

[47] 1 Timothy 1:12-14: "I thank him who has given me strength, Christ Jesus our Lord, because he judged me faithful, appointing me to his service, though formerly I was a blasphemer, persecutor, and insolent opponent. But I received mercy because I had acted ignorantly in unbelief, and the grace of our Lord overflowed for me with the faith and love that are in Christ Jesus."

4) Lord, what are some of my natural proclivities, habits, and giftings? (You can consider an assessment like the CliftonStrengths® assessment.)

5) Lord, what are some ways You want me to walk in the fullness of my character?

You make decisions every day, which is a part of the beauty of being human. You can determine that you will do activities that honor God or decide to do things that dishonor God. It's your choice. For instance, if you wanted to get up 30 minutes earlier tomorrow to meet with the Lord to read, journal, and pray, you could. If you wanted to take a break in the middle of your day for 15 minutes to pause, meditate on scripture, and pray, you could. Or, if before you lay your head down at night, you decided to put away your technology, sit at the side of your bed, raise your hands in praise to the Lord, and worship Him for who He is, you could.

There is **nothing** stopping you from making decisions to honor the Lord. We must all stop making excuses.

Consider these scriptures in the New Testament that are explicit in their focus on God's agenda. Notice how each of them requires a decision.

1. A Decision to Fellowship

    God is faithful, by whom you were called into the fellowship of His Son, Jesus Christ our Lord (1 Corinthians 1:9).

Fellowship requires more than one person, and both parties need to decide and agree. For any of us to continue in a relationship, we have to make regular decisions. We must choose to forgive. We have to determine if we need to overlook an offense. We must conclude how we will view the other. We need to establish an emotional climate to welcome healthy conversation, and we have to work through our agreements on values, ethics, and belief systems. Each of the above is needed to proceed forward in various relational circumstances.

The same principles of relationship-building apply to our connection with God. We have to make regular relational decisions. Jesus tells His followers that if they desire a relationship with Him, they must deny their lives, take up their crosses daily, and follow Him. Also, consider the words of Amos 3:3, "Do two walk together, unless they have agreed to meet?"

In this first area of decision-making, **have you decided to agree with God in His calling to fellowship with you?**

2. A Decision to Sacrifice

> I appeal to you therefore, brothers and sisters, by the mercies of God, to present your bodies as a living sacrifice, holy and acceptable to God, which is your spiritual worship. Do not be conformed to this world, but be transformed by the renewal of your mind, that by testing you may discern what is the will of God, what is good and acceptable and perfect (Romans 12:1-2).

Sacrifices are the currency of the spiritual realm. The spiritual world, in general, requires a sacrificial exchange with humans to release its spiritual benefits to the natural world. God created all things, and humans decided to rebel against God's created order. God chose to fix the disconnection between God and humans through the good news of Jesus' death, burial, and resurrection. Because God chose to fix the problem, it is reasonable for humans to offer themselves to God, since Jesus paid our debt for sin and satisfied God's requirements. In simple, God gives grace to humans in exchange for the sacrifice of Jesus. Because of Jesus' sacrifice, we are invited to offer our lives to God because of the payment made on our behalf.

On the contrary, evil demonic spirits of fear, pride, perversion, and rejection demand a constant exchange of human blood, time, money, talents, purpose, and resources in deceitful exchange for their "benefits" of magic, notoriety, praise from humans, power, prestige, false freedom, self-sufficiency, or ungodly gain. Demonic spirits constantly lurk, demand, oppress, and depress humans, requiring increasingly endless and unfulfilling sacrifices. Demons will continually demand an ongoing exchange, while God made only one exchange by paying for our sins through Jesus' life. God places the weight on Jesus' work. Demons place the weight on human effort. God's exchange is not burdensome, and it gives us new life, while demonic exchanges are deadly and keep us in bondage.

In this second area of decision-making, **have you decided to give your life as a sacrifice to the Lord instead of giving yourself to everything else?**

3. A Decision to Abstain

> For this is the will of God, your sanctification: that you abstain from sexual immorality; that each one of you know how to control his own body in holiness and honor, not in the passion of lust like the

> Gentiles who do not know God; that no one transgress and wrong his brother in this matter, because the Lord is an avenger in all these things, as we told you beforehand and solemnly warned you. For God has not called us for impurity, but in holiness. Therefore whoever disregards this, disregards not man but God, who gives his Holy Spirit to you (1 Thessalonians 4:3-5).

We can make decisions to put away things of our sinful nature, since the Lord's agenda is to grow us up into the maturity of our faith. He does not want us to remain in our past state, which is dead in our sins, but to experience the new life that God has given to us through the death, burial, and resurrection of Jesus. To abstain is not a demand on your humanity to make it happen by your power, but it is an empowerment given to you by God's Holy Spirit.

If you have decided to allow Jesus' sacrifice - His death, burial, and resurrection - to be the payment for your human brokenness and sins, then you have received the Holy Spirit of God. Holy Spirit can teach you about everything and remind you of what Jesus has said to you. Holy Spirit can convict you of your wrongdoing, your true identity, and God's upcoming judgment. Holy Spirit will also counsel, comfort, and help you on your journey toward wholeness. In other words, your belief in Jesus' death, burial, and resurrection has given you the benefits of overcoming your old life. You are free to live a new life!

In this third area of decision-making, **have you decided to let Holy Spirit help you overcome your old life?**

THE ULTIMATE GOAL OF DECIDING TOWARD THE WILL OF GOD

The Bible starts with the creation story of how God created order on the planet. He established everything in a certain way to sustain life. One part of this process is that humans were designed for fellowship and communion with God. That was broken when sin entered the world.

God went on a quest to restore the broken connection with Himself and humanity, deciding to come in human form to fix the issue through Jesus' life. Jesus represented the fullness of God in bodily form. The ultimate goal, therefore, is that God wants the restoration of fellowship and communion with you and me. He desires a Garden of Eden experience for us.

PRACTICAL LISTENING PRAYER QUESTIONS FOR THE DEPARTMENT OF WILL

1) Lord, where are some places in my life where I am in bondage?

2) Lord, how have I sacrificed parts of my life to this bondage?

3) Lord, who is the evil spirit that has placed me in bondage?

4) Lord, how do I break the agreement and decide toward Your will for my life?

5) Lord, what else do You want to share with me about the decisions and sacrifices I've made?

I want to end by giving you a plethora of other questions you can ask the Lord. The journey is to live this life with a whole, integrated heart, and I prefer that we end by giving the Lord the final say. I am always reminded that our hearts are His creation, not ours. He always knows best.

I appreciate you, and I hope this revelation has changed your perspective on your heart. It has changed mine.

Remember that according to Proverbs 20:5, you can become a person of understanding to draw out the depths of the purposes of your heart. God can and will show you how to do this as you seek Him. Please go and enjoy fellowship with the King of the Universe, and may you glorify the Lord in all that you do!

ADDITIONAL QUESTIONS TO ASK THE LORD

For the questions below, you can bring them to the Lord multiple times and in various seasons. Please recognize that these questions are simply conversation starters between you and the Lord. The goal is not just to get an answer and move on in life, but to invite you into a bigger, deeper relationship with the Lord. He is one who will give you understanding that reveals the purposes of your heart. Allow Him to show you the depths of your heart's functionality. Again, the questions below are a way to begin exploring certain areas of your heart.

Development of Your Least-Developed Departments:

- Which department(s) of my heart are least developed?
- What has caused the lack of development?
- What are some things I can do to develop these department(s)?
- What are some scriptural references to meditate on as I grow and change?
- What else do I need to know about this development process?

Development of Your Most-Developed Departments:

- What department of my heart is most developed?
- How did this development happen?
- Are there renovations You desire to do in this department?
- What are ways You are glorified when I display this part of my heart to the world?
- What else do I need to know about this development process?

Integration Across Your Heart Departments

- How do my heart departments work together?
- How do I intentionally integrate my heart departments?
- What strategies do You have for me to keep my departments integrated?
- How have I used certain departments to hide, cover up, or minimize other departments?
- What else do You need me to know?

Hidden Areas of Your Heart Departments

- Will You expose any hidden areas in any of my heart departments?
- What is being exposed, and what do I do to deal with it?
- Why was it hidden?
- What are some strategies to help me keep from hiding this again?
- What else do You need me to know?

Guarding Your Heart

- What are some ways that I do not guard, keep, or protect my heart according to Proverbs 4:23?
- What has trained these patterns of not guarding, keeping, or protecting?
- What are some new patterns for me?
- What are the benefits of the new patterns?
- What else do You need me to know?

Community Influences

- Who are some trustworthy people in my life with whom I can express and share my heart?
- What part(s) of my life can I share with them?
- What do I need to know about each person holistically and individually?
- How do I share things with them?
- What else do I need to know about the community You have given to me?

Spiritual Influences

- For each of my heart departments, who are the ruling spirit(s) that lead the department?
- How have I sacrificed toward these spirit(s)?
- What do You want me to do to renounce, disassociate, and/or deal with the sacrifices I made?
- What is a better way for me?
- What else do I need to know about the spiritual influences on my heart?

Other Miscellaneous Questions

Use these questions to **continually** invite the Lord to speak to you.

- What else do You want me to know?
- Where else do You want to explore with me?
- Who else do You want to partner with me in this journey?
- What's the goal of all of this for me, Lord?
- What else do You want to say?

Chapter Seventeen

IMPORTANT REMINDERS AND NEXT STEPS

Friend, you made it! Well done!

My hope is that this work has provided you with a framework for viewing your heart through a new lens, one that differs from some of the more widely accepted perspectives. I trust you are hungrier than ever to explore the depths of what's happening inside of you.

IMPORTANT REMINDERS

Here are some reminders after reading this book:

The purposes of your heart are deep.

> The purpose in a man's heart is like deep water, but a man of understanding will draw it out (Proverbs 20:5).

Your understanding comes from intimacy with the Lord.

> The fear of the Lord is the beginning of wisdom, and the knowledge of the Holy One is insight [understanding] (Proverbs 9:10).

Protect, keep, and guard your heart, which is like the central headquarters of your life.

> Keep your heart with all vigilance, for from it flow the springs of life (Proverbs 4:23).

Each statement above points to the importance of how we learn about what's happening inside our hearts. You will need understanding. You will need to know the Lord, the Holy One. You will need to keep and protect your heart. Please don't neglect to do the intentional, hard work of allowing the Lord to show you what's happening inside of you.

NEXT STEPS

A book like this is not just for you to increase your intellect with another Christian book and then set it aside. It is designed for you to start engaging more deeply with God about what's happening inside you. It's also designed to awaken your perspective of what God has for you.

I encourage you to go back and review the journaling exercises throughout the book, asking the Lord more questions. He loves to speak.

I encourage you to share your insights with your brothers and sisters and to have them buy a copy of the book for themselves, or you give one away as a gift to them.

I encourage you to do group Bible studies with your community and to collectively seek God about how to grow more intimate in your relationship with Him and with each other.

Spend more time with the Lord by letting Holy Spirit be your primary teacher. He will bring other trustworthy brothers and sisters into your life who can help draw out the best in you.

If feasible, invite Davies & Associates to speak to your church, Bible study fellowship, or ministry to encourage you in your journey to see your heart reconciled with the Lord. We'd love to encourage you.

Please do not hesitate to reach out for some additional training and coaching.

I hope all the best for you. I would love to pray as we conclude:

> *Lord, You know our hearts.*
>
> *Holy Spirit, I ask You to rest on us with power.*
>
> *Give us a spirit of wisdom and understanding, a spirit of counsel and might, and a spirit of knowledge and the fear of the Lord. Help us to delight in the fear of the Lord.*
>
> *I ask that You sustain and keep my friend on this journey of knowing You, loving You, and allowing You to lead them.*
>
> *Lord, teach them Your ways.*

Lord, bless them and keep them. Turn Your face toward them and be gracious to them. Lift up Your countenance toward them and grant them Your peace.

May Your peace that surpasses all understanding, guard their heart in the knowledge of Jesus.

Show them the purposes of their hearts, Lord.

I ask these things, and I bless them in Jesus' name!

Your Brother and Friend,

Dr. Conrad A. Davies
Email: conrad@daviesassociatesllc.com

Davies & Associates, LLC
Training & Coaching
http://daviesassociatesllc.com

Be Reconciled Lexington, Inc.
501(c)(3) Nonprofit Organization
http://bereconciledlexington.org

www.ingramcontent.com/pod-product-compliance
Lightning Source LLC
LaVergne TN
LVHW010625100826
845148LV00014B/3110
* 9 7 9 8 9 8 5 4 9 2 1 2 5 *